This book is dedicated to my wife, Carla, for her undying love and support; to my daughter, Lucidity, "the kid ghost hunter;" to my mom and dad, to my paranormal research crew, and to all my friends. You are all greatly appreciated.

*This book is in memory of
Gerald Eugene Trenum, Sr.
January 20, 1939–May 19, 2012
"The greatest storyteller of them all."*

True Casefiles of a

PARANORMAL

INVESTIGATOR

About the Author

Stephen Lancaster (Little River, SC) is a paranormal researcher who has been investigating ghosts since 1997. He is the producer of *MonsterVisionTV*, an independent paranormal investigation program with nearly two million views worldwide. In 2011, he began hosting the paranormal radio show "Shadowalker Radio" at Liveparanormal.com. His extreme horror documentary *Monstrosity* will be released in 2012. Visit him online at StephenLancaster.com.

To Write to the Author

If you wish to contact the author or would like more information about this book, please write to the author in care of Llewellyn Worldwide, and we will forward your request. Both the author and publisher appreciate hearing from you and learning of your enjoyment of this book and how it has helped you. Llewellyn Worldwide cannot guarantee that every letter written to the author can be answered, but all will be forwarded. Please write to:

Stephen Lancaster
℅ Llewellyn Worldwide
2143 Wooddale Drive
Woodbury, MN 55125-2989

Please enclose a self-addressed stamped envelope for reply, or $1.00 to cover costs. If outside the USA, enclose an international postal reply coupon.

True Casefiles of a
PARANORMAL
INVESTIGATOR

Stephen Lancaster

Llewellyn Publications
Woodbury, Minnesota

True Casefiles of a Paranormal Investigator © 2012 by Stephen Lancaster. All rights reserved. No part of this book may be used or reproduced in any manner whatsoever, including Internet usage, without written permission from Llewellyn Publications, except in the case of brief quotations embodied in critical articles and reviews.

FIRST EDITION
First Printing, 2012

Book design by Bob Gaul
Cover art: Ghost house © iStockphoto.com/Giorgio Fochesato
          Man © iStockphoto.com/Dan Wilton
Cover design by Kevin R. Brown
Editing by Lee Lewis Walsh

Llewellyn Publications is a registered trademark of Llewellyn Worldwide Ltd.

Library of Congress Cataloging-in-Publication Data (Pending)
978-0-7387-3220-6

Llewellyn Worldwide Ltd. does not participate in, endorse, or have any authority or responsibility concerning private business transactions between our authors and the public.

All mail addressed to the author is forwarded, but the publisher cannot, unless specifically instructed by the author, give out an address or phone number.

Any Internet references contained in this work are current at publication time, but the publisher cannot guarantee that a specific location will continue to be maintained. Please refer to the publisher's website for links to authors' websites and other sources.

Llewellyn Publications
A Division of Llewellyn Worldwide Ltd.
2143 Wooddale Drive
Woodbury, MN 55125-2989
www.llewellyn.com

Printed in the United States of America

Contents

Introduction

I am more fascinated with those who are dead than those who are alive. I know how the living work, but it is the dead that truly fascinate me. My name is Stephen David Lancaster II and I am a paranormal researcher, searching for an answer to that age-old question about life carrying on after death.

In 1987, when I was a child, a violent and unseen force attacked me. That one event gave birth to my interest in this unique line of work. In 1997, I began searching for an answer to my own questions about that terrifying night.

After a few years, my crusade shifted to helping others with their paranormal encounters and experiences, because the more I could be exposed to potential spiritual energy, the closer I would be to solving the mystery. In fourteen years, I have researched and investigated hundreds of cases involving paranormal phenomena.

My research has been recognized nationally on television programs, on radio broadcasts, in magazines, and in countless other publications. The work I have conducted and the evidence I have gathered has appeared on NBC, CBS, and the A&E network show *Biography*.

In 2007, the demand for my research and investigative talents became overwhelming and I could no longer handle the workload. I needed to figure out a way to make the research more productive, more accessible, and more available. I decided to assemble a team. I created the P.I.T. Crew, which is short for Paranormal Investigation Team. Initially, the team consisted of just a few investigators. Over the years, it has expanded to include dozens of members. In 2008, the P.I.T. Crew became the subject of a paranormal investigation program called *Monstervision TV*.

So how do I conduct paranormal research? Is it like you see on television? Sometimes, but not entirely. The equipment I use certainly plays a pivotal role in validating extraordinary claims. Without these tools, proving and disproving paranormal occurrences would be difficult to achieve—especially the disproving part.

The most commonly used tool is the video camera. Visual proof of a ghost is what most involved in this field view as the Holy Grail of evidence. While digital formats are readily available, I continue to document with video cameras that record on film. That often is quite shocking to those who have welcomed the digital age with open arms. However, film can be validated. Film can be analyzed for authenticity. Digital formats cannot.

The same can be said for photography. Still-shot, film cameras are used at great length during any given investigation; however, we also use digital cameras.

Audio recorders are next in line as far as importance is concerned; recording audio is vital when communicating with what is believed to be a spirit. Once again, I prefer a format that can be validated and use cassette tapes instead of digital recording formats. Electronic voice phenomena (EVP) are among the most commonly reported pieces of evidence. An EVP occurs when a disembodied voice is discovered on a recording. These voices were not heard during the time of recording and are later discovered during playback.

The electromagnetic field (EMF) tester is another staple in the arsenal of paranormal research tools. Contrary to popular belief, this device is mostly utilized as a tool to disprove a haunting, rather than to prove it. EMF testers or detectors measure the amount of electromagnetic fields in any given area. A K-2 meter is a similar tool used for the same purpose.

Electrical devices such as refrigerators, fuse boxes, and alarm clocks omit a very high level of EMFs. Hallucinations, nausea, and paranoia can occur in an individual overly exposed to these excessive fields. In other words, what was once believed to have been a ghost could have been nothing more than a delusion created by overexposure to EMFs.

However, it is believed that spirits can use such fields to gather energy for manifesting, communicating, or moving objects. An EMF is typically stationary within the environment creating it, so it is highly unusual to track and locate one that is actually moving throughout an area. This could point to spiritual intervention.

As an extension to both the EMF detector and audio recorder, I use a tool called an electromagnetic pickup to further validate findings from both devices. This instrument allows the user to hear the sound magnetic fields create. The louder the sound, the stronger the field. The sound can best be described as white noise or static. In theory, one could be able to hear a spirit communicating in real time, as opposed to discovering a voice later as an EVP.

Temperature-reading devices further the research by monitoring and documenting sudden and dramatic changes in the surrounding environment. Colder areas or cold spots have been attributed to spiritual activity when the area was measured prior to the sudden change.

Ambient and laser are the two most frequently used versions of the thermometer. Ambient thermometers are great for monitoring a central area, typically where the investigator is located, whereas laser thermometers are useful for monitoring areas that are unreachable in a desired time frame, or unreachable entirely. Laser thermometers use a beam similar to a laser pointer for detecting the temperature of an area or surface farther away from the investigator.

A unique piece of equipment I use regularly is the MV-1 goggles. Only one pair exists. I custom-designed them based on my theory that spirits can be seen in a light spectrum typically invisible to the naked eye. They are fashioned with special lenses that allow the wearer to see the 720-nanometer light spectrum, which is within the infrared spectrum.

Standard infrared cameras or goggles allow an individual to see in pure darkness, a technology called night vision. However, the MV-1 goggles permit an individual to see the light that infrared radiation creates. In other words, one would only see pure black when looking through the MV-1 unless something in the 720-nanometer light spectrum entered the viewing area. When observing an area believed to contain spiritual activity through the goggles, the user may see anomalies in a deep red color, or occasionally in pure white.

There are many other instruments used in paranormal research, but most of those find their place when a particular situation calls for it. New devices and investigative techniques continue to surface in the mainstream as knowledge and awareness grows.

Credible, respected, and serious paranormal researchers will tell you that the investigative work goes far beyond any one location, experience, occurrence, or specialized tool. Answers cannot be found in a matter of just a few hours. Having thorough documentation of each investigation and piece of evidence is crucial. That is where the case files become a reference point for future work. Case files contain the stories, the history, the findings, and in some cases, the proof that we do not walk this earth alone.

This book contains some of the most productive cases I have researched throughout the years, in search of an answer to a question I first asked twenty-five years ago: *are ghosts real?* These are true accounts of the paranormal from a professional researcher and investigator.

1 BIRTH OF A PARANORMAL INVESTIGATOR

Tall tales and big-fish stories are the backbone of every small town. It never seems to fail and most definitely never ceases to amaze me—there's always an unbelievable story from the most unreliable source. Whether it be from the stereotypical town drunk; the crazy, old, wrinkled-up, sunken-eyed, should-be-dead widow from the rundown haunted mansion on the hill; the bored old man with a knack for theatrics who has nothing better to do than to convince children of stuff that never happened; or the children themselves with their limitless imaginations—every town has its story. And every time, it seems like that story comes from one of the sources described above.

You have to wonder sometimes if there was ever some miniscule piece of truth in all those far-fetched tales you heard around the campfire as a kid. I have always wondered that. I have heard my share of the unbelievable, there is no question about it. In fact, I seek it.

My grandfather always seemed to get my eyes gazing every time I was at his house, stuffing my face with my grandmother's dippy eggs, with some crazy story about an axe killer who still lurks about, or a swamp creature that eats little blonde-haired and blue-eyed children. You guessed right: I have blonde hair and blue eyes. Go figure.

I remember two houses down, an old lady lived in what appeared to be vines with a roof. The house was old, patched together, and thankfully for her, we never had a hurricane season. This old lady was different. She was a witch—a real witch. My neighbors had filled my head time and time again with this nonsense, and rationally, I did not believe it. I wanted to, but I did not.

My brother and I had a friend living next door to us. The kid had warts all over his right hand. His dad suggested we go see the witch. (I swear to you, I am not making this up.) Our friend asked me and my brother to go with him to her house. We did, very cautiously. We knocked on the door and a man appeared, asking us what we wanted. We proceeded to tell him we were there to see the witch about our friend's warts. Long story short, she came out onto the porch, licked her old bony fingers, and started touching his right hand while saying some jargon I could not even begin to spell. When she was done, we left.

The next day our friend came pounding on my door, screaming at the top of his lungs. The warts were gone. That's the kind of town I grew up in.

My hometown: land of wart-ridding witches, swamp monsters, lurking killers, and giant turtles. Did I leave out the giant turtles? Do not let me dwell on that, but we had a three-foot-high, five-foot-long giant turtle chained to a tree—yes, chained—up in the woods outside an old farmhouse. At night it would bellow at the moon like a werewolf or something. I wish you could hear me recreating the sound it made. Weird. As the story goes, the thing ate dogs. Sounds unbelievable, doesn't it? Like I said, that's the kind of town I grew up in.

I'm surprised the movie industry has not tapped my hometown. I grew up there; I saw this stuff firsthand, and the stories I heard almost always had some truth to them. I know, because I sought it out. This book is no different—well, I guess it is, in a way. There is no psychotic axe murderer living in the abandoned silk mill or slime-oozing leech man from the Green Swamp. No giant bellowing dog-eating turtles or twenty-four-hour wart removal programs.

As a kid, I always loved hearing these old stories from my grandfather, my father, or the local loon, and I always wondered at what point I would have stories to tell myself. This is where my story begins.

———————

My hometown, Lonaconing, is buried in the mountains of western Maryland. Population was around one thousand, let's say. Hunters, fisherman, coaches, men who slaved sixteen hours a day at the paper mill, neighbors who knew your business and made it their job to know it. People lived behind unlocked doors, among thousands of the greenest of trees that, come autumn, would be any painter's dream. The daily trains exporting coal from the heart of the surrounding mountains seemed to shake and shift the entire town every time they passed. Personally, I was fond of the sound. I loved lying down, closing my eyes, and falling under the hypnotic spell of the trains' rhythm. There was something very therapeutic about that.

Trees and animals outnumbered the people in the town and it was nothing to see our local black bears break up a Tuesday night Little League game. I was always happy to see them; I hated baseball. Hell, I hated all sports, but I played them anyway. So having my big black furry friends end the game a bit early always put a smile on my face. The town was named after some old Native American tribe. We actually had our own t-shirts with "wherethehellislonaconing?" written across the front.

In 1987, I lived in Lonaconing with my parents and my younger brother in a typical American home in a typical American neighborhood. But the house we were living in, according to a few neighbors, had a somewhat atypical history. I remember one neighbor in particular telling me that an old man who previously lived in the house was found dead in the attic of an apparent suicide. At the time, I did not think anything of this story. It was not something that really bothered me. Looking back, I wish I had dug a little deeper into these claims.

I was ten years old in 1987 and my younger brother was five. Sleeping in bunk beds, we shared a bedroom. As the older brother, I felt it fitting that I slept on the top bunk. I called it: that meant it was mine, and my brother had no choice but to accept sleeping on the bottom bunk.

It was December, and I can vividly recall the winter chill. Our house was heated by a coal furnace, with heat that could never quite reach our bedroom. It always seemed a little bit colder on that top bunk, and I suppose that was the downside of staking claim to it. Our parents slept across the hall in their own room.

We had not been living in the house for very long at this point. If I remember correctly, this was going to be our first holiday season there. Over the previous few months, nothing out of the ordinary was noticed by any of us, to my knowledge. If strange things were occurring in the house prior to my experience, it would have been news to me.

On December 14, 1987, in the safety of my home, I was attacked by something I could not see. That night is so clear to me that I can actually recall those events more accurately than something that happened only a few months ago.

The night started off like any other. Everything was normal. My brother and I were always supposed to be ready for bed by nine o'clock. That did not mean he or I actually went to bed at that time. We did, however, humor our folks and pretend to sleep until we knew they were out of potential range of hearing us. After playing around like mischievous brothers do, we finally decided it was time for bed.

My brother could always fall asleep almost on cue. It was uncanny. However, I always struggled with sleep, as I do even today. But I eventually felt my eyes getting heavy and fell asleep around one o'clock. Approximately an hour and a half later, I was awakened abruptly by something pulling on my ankles in a timid yet playful fashion. Naturally, the first thing that came to mind was that my little brother was messing around. I leaned over the railing of the top bunk, stretching my head out to where I could see him underneath, on his bed. He appeared to be fast asleep. Even so, I dismissed it as him playing a joke and decided to just go back to sleep.

As I dozed off, once again something started pulling on my ankles. This time the tugging was a little harder. Once again, I leaned over the railing of the top bunk in an attempt to catch my brother pulling a prank. Just like moments earlier, he appeared to be sound asleep.

Now I began questioning whether it was, in fact, my brother playing a joke. The speed at which he would've had to move, to pull on my ankles and immediately be lying still in apparent slumber, was nearly impossible. There was no sound coming from underneath me. Still sitting up in bed, confused by the situation, I noticed my blanket slowly being pulled toward the bottom of the bed. For the third time, I quickly threw my head over the top bunk railing to where I could see my brother, and, amazingly, he still appeared to be fast asleep.

I was now even more confused as to what could have been pulling on me from the bottom of the bed. I leaned down to start pulling my blanket back up when, shockingly, an invisible force wrapped itself around both of my wrists. Imagine someone grabbing you around the wrists. You know what that feels like. This felt exactly like that. Something was holding on to me and not letting go. The skin around my wrists was actually indented, as if someone were physically grabbing me. Only in this case, I couldn't see this someone with the naked eye. I was experiencing my first paranormal encounter with an unknown entity.

Completely in fear, I attempted to pull away and break free from this invisible restraint. It seemed like the more I fought against this entity, the stronger and more violent it got. My entire body felt weak. Within seconds, all of my bodily energy had been drained. The entity continued to pull my wrists toward the bottom of the bed. One violent pull lifted me from a sitting position, completely flipping my body. My head was now at the bottom of the bed with my arms stretched out, still held involuntarily by this being. My feet were now where my pillow was. I had been forced to flip positions on the bed.

Terrified, I attempted to scream for my parents. I had no power and no energy and nothing would come out of my mouth that made any audible sense. I can remember hearing straining gasps in place of *Mom* and *Dad*, the words I was attempting to scream. I just could not get anything out. I continued to pull and fight this unknown and unseen power. Then, in an unpredictable moment, I broke free.

I had been pulling and fighting so hard that once the entity finally let go of my wrists, the sudden lack of resistance caused me to fly across the bed, smashing the back of my head into the wall. I hit the wall so hard that an impression was left in the wood paneling. At that point, my bodily energy returned and I was able to scream at the top of my lungs one word: "Mom!"

It was only a matter of seconds before my parents' bedroom light came on, followed by the hall light just outside my room. They rushed into the room in a panic, concerned about the commotion. At this point, the excitement roused my brother from his slumber. The entire family had all eyes on me. Covered in sweat and still emotionally distraught, I recounted the strange events that had occurred just moments earlier. Considering my age and the odd situation, my parents did what most would have done, and dismissed the entire event as a nightmare.

The events of that night molded the adult I would later become. Something undeniably paranormal happened to me, and I made it my mission to find the answers to the many questions that event raised in my mind. From that point forward, I became intrigued with the paranormal. I started reading about parapsychology, UFO sightings and alien abductions, possessions, clairvoyance, ghost sightings, extrasensory perception, cryptozoology, exorcisms, and just about anything I could get my hands on that covered the unexplained. Growing up in a Christian home made it very difficult to openly discuss such topics. In most cases, the reading material I was interested in had to be brought into the house in a very covert manner.

Over the next few years, I did my best to keep my interest in and passion for the unknown a secret from my family.

My experience with that ghost was not the last time something unexplainable happened in that house. A few years later, my brother and I had broken free from the bunk beds and we each had our own room. I remember one night waking up to the sound of a baby crying. This was quite odd, considering my brother and I were the only children in the house at the ages of thirteen and eight.

Since I grew up in a very musical home, I was lucky enough to have a full drum set in my bedroom, along with guitars and keyboards. The drum set was handed down to me by my father, so it was quite dated at that point, but still kicked. The sound of a baby crying was coming from the other side of my room near the drums; specifically, from around the bass pedal area behind the bass drum. I felt no fear and quickly jumped out of bed and ran over to where the sound was coming from.

As I leaned over the tom drums mounted on top of the bass drum, I saw a nearly transparent baby lying on the floor. Once his eyes made contact with mine, the crying stopped. Now I did feel afraid and quickly ran back across the room, leaping into my bed. I stayed still for about ten minutes until my curiosity got the better of me. I went back over to look for the mysterious infant. To my surprise, he was gone. Looking back, that incident could have easily been a dream, although I do not believe it was.

Paranormal activity seemed to occur in the house every three years, and only for one night. The first time, I was ten and the second time, I was thirteen. Both occurrences were completely different from each other. One was violent, while the other was not. And like clockwork, three years later there was another incident in the house—only this time I was not the only one who witnessed it.

I was sixteen and my brother was eleven. We were playing outside with a neighborhood friend. It was summer, so our parents were at work and we were left at home to do what kids do over the break from school. My brother and I, along with our friend, were around the back of the house when this third occurrence took place.

The bedroom that my brother and I had once shared was now his. Six years had passed without incident in that room. As the three of us were playing around outside, my brother glanced up at his bedroom window. He screamed my name, claiming somebody was standing in the window looking down at us. As I looked up to see what he was talking about, the window shattered, throwing glass down onto the grass where we stood. Although I never actually saw the anomalous figure my brother was so adamant about seeing, I did witness the glass shattering before my eyes. Our neighbor friend also said he saw the window shatter.

This all happened within seconds and, before anybody could say anything, I was halfway into the house and up the stairs to investigate. When I arrived at my brother's bedroom, I was really surprised to see that not a single shard of glass had fallen in the room. I was looking for a rock, or any object really, that could have broken that glass from the outside. There was nothing to be found. The window had shattered from the inside out. That was truly remarkable.

Moments later, my brother and our friend arrived in the bedroom. They too, were dumbfounded as to how the window could have shattered. Of course, what made this situation more difficult to handle was the fact that we had to somehow explain this to our father without sounding like we had gone off the deep end. Long story short, we never did tell him the truth. We simply said it was an accident on our part.

We moved from that house before the next three-year mark came, so I never knew if the paranormal activity occurred again. I did at one point try to revisit the house, but the people who bought it from my parents never seemed to be home when I stopped by.

———

I left Maryland in 1999, after college, and didn't return until March 2010. My research and involvement in the paranormal community was never discussed during phone calls with my folks. Finally, after I returned, my parents and I shared many discussions about the paranormal, my career, and upcoming projects. But one conversation in particular really opened my eyes to the reality of what had happened to me over two decades ago.

In 1987, my parents had dismissed my experience as a nightmare. Little did I know, however, that they were keeping some things secret. During a conversation about that night, my mother decided to share certain truths that I had never before heard. She explained to me that the exact same thing had happened to her when she was ten years old. My mouth dropped to the floor.

Of course, when I was a child, my mother did not want to scare me by telling the truth. As a father myself, I completely understand that. Her experience was slightly more violent than mine, however. Whatever attacked her actually left visible marks around her wrists. Her experience shared many similarities with mine, like the violent pulling and throwing and her bodily energy being drained. She was awakened abruptly from sleep just as I was.

I am not sure why marks were not left on me. Maybe I was stronger and pulled free sooner, but I will never know for sure. It was certainly interesting to hear about my mother's experience. That added more validity to what happened to me.

So there you have it. These were the experiences that ultimately caused me to become heavily involved in the paranormal field. One house with three separate and seemingly unrelated unexplainable occurrences changed my entire perception of reality. They say certain events in your childhood are the key ingredients that make who you are in adulthood. My life has proven there is much truth to that statement.

2 MY OUIJA EXPERIENCE

Ten years had passed since I first shook hands with a ghost. At this point in my life, I was in the middle of my second year of college. During that time I worked two different jobs. The first one was a part-time gig at a West Virginia–based classic rock radio station called Q94. I was a morning disc jockey filling in for one of the regulars who happened to be on extended leave. I was also a camp counselor for a local high school.

At the age of nineteen, I was the youngest of the camp counselors—in fact, the youngest after me was in his forties. I was only two years out of high school and managed to get roped into chaperoning the camp attendees. Truth be told, it was a favor for my old music teacher. As one of the head counselors, he was in need of help for that summer. Honestly, I did not mind, considering I could still relate to the students. Hell, I was only two to three years older than most of them.

We were to spend a week in the mountains of West Virginia for a field trip of sorts. The camp was pretty lame and I speak for most when I say the fun was had after everybody supposedly went to bed. Each night I would leave the counselors' cabin and head over to the boys' cabin, just to keep them in check. It was not uncommon to find the old "pillows under the blanket" trick being pulled in an attempt by the boys to sneak into the girls' cabin.

I was the "cool" guy who could somehow pull off chaperoning them without chaperoning them. They considered me to be one of the guys and I appreciated that. Of course, that also helped me keep them out of trouble and, believe me, they needed to be kept out of trouble. For some reason those kids thought that was cool. Who was I to argue?

I remember that week vividly. My most haunting memory and the sole topic of this chapter was my first and last Ouija board experience.

My experience with the Ouija board opened my eyes to a realm of paranormal research I had yet to explore. I was curious about it for sure. Up until this point, I had never been in a situation to use one. People had always told me about crazy sessions they'd had with the board, but I mostly listened in disbelief, having never witnessed this phenomenon.

We were about halfway through the week at camp. I was doing my rounds as usual that night—checking in on the girls and the boys and walking around the entire camp, making sure everything was locked up and everybody was where they were supposed to be. I always checked on the boys last during my rounds, since I would spend a few hours with them each night. I typically arrived at their cabin around eleven.

Upon my arrival that evening, one of the students mentioned that he had brought a Ouija board with him to have something for everybody to do. At first I tried to shut down the idea. I was attempting to be the responsible one, suggesting that the other counselors and even the kids' parents might not approve of such a thing. I tried to explain to them how irresponsible I would look if something negative were to happen. I was trying to get the point across that having me as a counselor was a good thing for them, since I was not anal like the rest of the chaperones. I told them that if I approved of this idea, I risked losing my job as their counselor.

Of course, they proceeded to bust my balls about it. Now I was the lame guy instead of Mr. Cool. Long story short, I finally caved and told them to keep their mouths shut about it for the rest of the week. I told them that if I heard one word about it from the other counselors, I would deny any knowledge of it and they would lose their "lights on" privileges after eleven at night the rest of the week.

After all, it was not that long ago that I was in their position, looking up to a counselor. I admitted to having been the orchestrator of many shenanigans in my day, so who was I to hold back these kids from some potential fun? I was going to be present, so if the situation escalated or got out of hand, I could simply pull the plug on the session and take the board with me. Boy, is there some irony to that statement, which you will understand a little later.

I personally had no intention of participating in their Ouija session. I was simply there to supervise. Although they tried to get me to join in, I respectfully declined. Little did I know at the time that my participation was inevitable.

The boys grabbed the board and sat cross-legged in an intimate circle in the center of the cabin. I sat down on one of the lower bunks directly behind them. Only five boys were participating in the so-called fun. The rest of them were either trying to sleep or watching from a distance.

To set the mood, they turned off all the lights and used two electric lanterns to light up the area they were sitting in. I was thinking to myself, "Here we go," very sarcastically. I never had any reason to believe the stories about Ouija boards. Up until that night, I thought it was nothing more than a board game to play with during childhood sleepovers.

Andy, the kid who brought the board, placed it on the floor in the center of their circle and gave brief instructions to everyone on how to use it. He advised anyone who participated to touch the planchette very lightly. The planchette is the indicator used on Ouija boards that moves to answer questions, either by spelling out a word, pointing to a number, or choosing "yes" or "no." There are also entering and exiting sections of the board, most commonly referred to as "hello" and "goodbye."

Andy started the session by asking if there were any spirits with us in the cabin. Honestly, for the first twenty minutes absolutely nothing happened. The planchette did not move an inch as he asked in multiple ways if a spirit would talk to us. Finally, he did get a response. The planchette slid across the board, pointing to "yes." To be honest, at that moment I believed Andy to be moving it, not some spirit. He then proceeded to ask whom we were talking to. The planchette moved to the letter "s" and stopped. He continued on with all of the other boys staring in amazement. I was still sitting on a lower bunk, trying not to laugh at this nonsense.

Andy asked if the spirit's name started with the letter "s." The planchette moved quickly to "no." He continued by asking what the letter "s" meant if it was not the spirit's name. The planchette moved to spell out an entire name this time:

S–T–E–P–H–E–N

As soon as the word was complete, I could not resist blurting out, "Bullshit!" My name is Stephen and this seemed like a typical bamboozle to get me involved with the foolish thing.

Andy assured me that he did not intentionally spell out my name as a joke. He was convinced something else did. Regardless, he did have my attention at that point. I asked him to go ahead and continue. He asked if the spirit's name was Stephen. The planchette moved directly to "no." He asked if the spirit knew that a Stephen was sitting in the room with them. The planchette quickly moved to "yes."

I jumped up and playfully yelled at Andy, telling him enough was enough with his little prank. It was not like he was spooking me or anything; it was just a little annoying since I firmly believed he was moving the planchette. I figured I could end this quickly by instructing him to ask a question that only I knew the answer to: the nature of my first paranormal experience, and my age when it occurred. Knowing very well that only three people in my life knew the answer to that question and none of them were present, I figured this would end the shenanigans abruptly. I was wrong.

Andy acknowledged my request and asked the alleged spirit at what age I had my first paranormal experience. The planchette quickly moved to "no." We all sat there in silence for a moment. I decided to call out Andy by continuing to blame him for controlling the answers. He was adamant in trying to convince me that he was not.

Andy continued and asked the question again. Just like before, "no" was the response. This was not answering my question and did nothing more than further my belief that this was all bologna. He then asked if the spirit wanted me to touch the board instead of him. The planchette quickly moved to "yes."

Out of frustration, I finally shouted, "All right!" I figured that the only way I was ever going to be fully convinced of this phenomenon was to experience it myself, so I finally agreed to participate in the Ouija session. I knew that with my hands on the planchette, whatever happened was not going to be because I moved it.

Andy moved over so I could sit down in the circle in front of the Ouija board. I placed my hands very lightly on the planchette. I cannot say for sure whether it was the atmosphere or their excitement that affected me, but when I placed my hands on that piece, I could have sworn I felt a slight vibration. It felt like a very light and continuous electrical shock. This was not painful at all and was very faint, but it was noticeable. I did not mention this to the kids.

Back to business, I returned to the question Andy had been trying to get answered. I asked the alleged spirit when my first paranormal experience was. I felt the planchette slowly start moving underneath my hands. I was barely touching the thing. I have to admit I was dumbfounded and blown away when the planchette spelled out the word "ten." Before I could say anything, it continued to move up into the right-hand corner of the board, stopping and hovering over the "moon" or "night" symbol.

These answers were correct. My first paranormal experience was at night when I was ten years old.

As I sat there, staring at my hands and the planchette hovering over the moon symbol, Andy asked me if that was the right answer. I hesitated at first, but then nodded my head slightly. As I looked around at the other boys, I saw genuine fear in their eyes. Part of me knew I should have stopped there, but another part of me wanted to know more. For some reason, I could not resist keeping my hands on the planchette. If I was really talking with a spirit, there might be a good possibility that the questions I had about my first paranormal experience could be answered.

Before I could ask another personal question, Andy asked me to find out the name of the spirit. I too was curious as to whom we were speaking with, if we were speaking with anyone at all. Sure, it was quite uncanny that the board answered my private question correctly, but I was still a little skeptical. For all I knew, I could have subconsciously moved the planchette to spell out what I wanted to see. I thought that was highly unlikely, however, considering I was typically quite in tune with my own motivations.

I asked the spirit to please identify itself. Without hesitation, the planchette started moving again and spelled out:

M–O–R–G–A–N–A

The name meant absolutely nothing to me, although I knew it was probably female. The other boys did not recognize it either. Next I asked if she could tell me more about what happened the night I was attacked. She quickly answered "no." I asked her if she even knew what had happened to me. She answered "yes."

My mind was racing. I really wanted to believe I was talking with a spirit. All the answers seemed to point in favor of that. I was extremely curious as to why Morgana was so adamant about me being on the board that night. How did she know about my first paranormal experience? Was it her? Was she simply reading my mind? Was tonight's experience related to my earlier experience? How and why was I feeling some form of energy coming off the planchette?

I finally got frustrated enough to raise my voice and playfully try to intimidate her. I told her that if she would not answer my questions, we were going to end the session and put the board away. The planchette moved instantly to "no," almost as if she was threatening me. Now I was really starting to feel uncomfortable.

I told Morgana I really wanted to know what had happened to me as a child. I wanted to know who it was, and why it happened. Despite my questions, the planchette did not move. With my hands still on it, I looked around at the boys and suggested we put this thing away. At that moment, the two electric lanterns started to flicker slightly. I remember clearly hearing one of the boys yell, "Holy crap! The lanterns are flickering!"

Now, that easily could have been the batteries dying, or some other electrical malfunction. However, considering the circumstance, I too was starting to believe there was something more than that happening. As we were watching the lanterns flicker, the planchette finally started moving again. Like before, it moved to "no."

Andy quickly said, "But you didn't ask a question." I looked at him and said that I did not ask a question out loud, but I did say something to myself. He asked me what I said, and I told him that in my mind I said, "It's time to put this thing away." Apparently Morgana was in my head and did not want me to stop.

As I was sitting there looking at my hands on the planchette, a feeling of nausea started to overcome me. I started feeling extremely lightheaded and honestly felt like I was going to vomit. Andy asked me if I was all right. He said my face was really pale and I was sweating a great deal. I told him that I thought I was going to be sick.

One of the other boys frantically yelled, "That's enough, guys, this is crazy!" Then one of the boys grabbed my arms in a panic and pulled my hands off the planchette. He pulled so hard that I fell backward and landed flat on my back. For some reason, I just could not let go of the damned thing. I could not voluntarily release myself from it and actually needed help.

A few things happened at that moment. When he pulled my hands free, the planchette slid off the board and onto the wooden floor of the cabin. At the same time, Andy was screaming at the top of his lungs, "You didn't close the session! You didn't close the session!" As I stared at the cabin ceiling, I could hear him, but it sounded really muffled, like he was yelling at me through a wall. What he was saying honestly meant nothing to me. Like I said before, I had never dabbled with a Ouija board prior to that night. How was I supposed to know the proper spiritual etiquette?

Andy was authentically upset that I was pulled from the board without closing the session properly. He apparently knew a lot more about it than I did and his anger showed that. He started yelling at everybody about it. Even the kids who had been trying to sleep this whole time woke up from the screaming.

Since I was lying on my back, still fighting the nauseated feeling, Andy extended his hand to help me up. He had calmed down a little and asked if I was all right. I told him that I was completely exhausted but the nauseated feeling had dissipated. He said, "Dude, I think you were about to be possessed." I snickered a little in disbelief and said, "I really have no clue what the hell just happened, Andy."

After everybody calmed down, I realized this had been going on for hours and it was now after two in the morning. I told the boys to pack it in and instructed Andy to keep that thing hidden for the rest of the week. He agreed without argument. I made sure the boys were all in their bunks before I exited the cabin.

I headed straight to the shower. For some reason, I felt a strong urge to stand under hot water. I felt dirty and sick. As I stood under the shower, the events from moments earlier kept repeating in my mind. Was that real? Was I just caught up in the moment? I really didn't know.

While I was showering, I could have sworn that somebody was talking in the shower room. The place was huge and could accommodate up to a dozen people at once. On one wall were about six toilets, three urinals, and a row of sinks. I was convinced that one of the boys had left his bunk, either to use the restroom or pull a prank on me. Considering what we had all witnessed earlier, I found it hard to believe one of them would pull a prank, given my current emotional state. That would be a good way to get your ass kicked, to put it bluntly.

I stood under the shower for about twenty minutes, occasionally hearing what sounded like somebody talking. I finally turned the shower off, wrapped a towel around my waist, and took a look around the shower and bathroom facility. I saw nobody. I quickly threw my clothes back on and did one last check on the boys before retiring to my bed. The boys were fast asleep.

I arrived at the counselors' cabin and slowly opened the door as quietly as possible so as not to wake the other counselors. I crawled into my lower bunk and stared at the underneath of the top bunk for the next hour. I rolled over on my stomach, placed my left arm under the pillow, and buried my face in it. I would be only guessing, but somewhere around four in the morning I finally fell asleep. The counselors were supposed to wake each morning at six, and meet in the mess hall to discuss the day's events and start preparing breakfast for the kids. That would give me just two hours of sleep. The alarm clocks started going off promptly at six o'clock. I woke up, still lying on my stomach with my face buried in the pillow and my left arm underneath it, the same position I had fallen asleep in. A few moments later, I felt something hard underneath the pillow. I remained still, without acknowledging the other counselors and without investigating what I was feeling.

I waited until everyone had left for the mess hall. Then I slowly started moving my left arm out from underneath the pillow, with my face still buried in it. I could feel that whatever was under there was just about the size of my pillow. I could tell that it was actually inside the pillowcase, as opposed to being directly underneath it.

I turned over so I was facing the underneath of the top bunk. I pulled the pillow out from underneath my head and held it in front of me. These pillows had a zipper on the side of the pillowcase to keep it from slipping off. Still lying on my back, I unzipped the pillowcase and stuck my hand in there to pull out the object.

I only had it about a quarter of the way out when I realized it was Andy's Ouija board. Immediately I jumped up and in turn smashed my head on the bottom of the top bunk. That hurt like hell, and I rolled off the bed and onto the floor, holding my head in pain. The pillow with the Ouija board sticking out of the case fell onto the bed.

After I got over the knock to the head, I pulled myself up and stood beside the bed. I could not believe what I was seeing. There was that irony I spoke of earlier. Did I actually bring the Ouija board with me? You can only imagine the questions that were racing through my mind at that moment. How in the hell did that board get into a zipped-up pillowcase without me knowing it? How could one of those boys have successfully entered the counselors' cabin without waking anybody up? How could one of them enter the cabin, unzip my pillowcase, shove in the Ouija board, zip it back up, and exit without waking me up? The answer is they could not.

That cabin was dark as could be at night. Without a flashlight, there was no way one of those boys could have done this. With a flashlight, the other counselors and I would have been awakened. So how did they do it? I really wanted there to be a logical answer to this. I'd had a very strange and upsetting session on the Ouija board just four or so hours earlier. Then I woke up to the haunting realization that it had somehow been placed inside my pillowcase. I wanted answers.

Maybe it was fear that fueled me. Maybe it was anger. I am just not sure. I grabbed the board in both hands and shoved my knee through it. I split it in half. I took the pieces to the Dumpster behind the mess hall and disposed of them.

The camp attendees were to rise at seven-thirty in the morning, but honestly, I did not care. Those boys were about to get a six-thirty wakeup call, because I had questions that needed answering. I stormed over to their cabin and threw the door open, causing it to slam against the wall. I saw a few of them squirm a little in their bunks, but my dramatic entrance was not enough to roust them.

I walked over to a boom box that one of the boys brought to camp. I turned the volume dial to the maximum and pushed play on the cassette deck. The tape in the deck was Aerosmith's *Get A Grip* album.

Aerosmith got the boys moving, and as they were throwing balled-up socks and pillows at me, I proceeded to tell them that I wanted to know who had pulled a prank on me last night. I will admit the look on all of their faces was not the look I wanted to see. They all looked confused. They were glancing around at one another, clueless as to what I was talking about. It was like they were all waiting for someone to come out and admit something, only nobody did.

I finally walked over to Andy and flat-out said, "'fess up, man." He looked at me with an empty stare. He had no clue what I was talking about. As I continued pacing around their cabin, I could tell they were getting a little antsy.

There were many thoughts racing through my mind. Should I tell them I found the Ouija board zipped up inside my pillowcase? What if they had nothing to do with it? Would I freak them out? What if they did have something to do with it and this was nothing more than a very elaborate prank, one that rivaled anything I had ever pulled off in my day? I mean, I had pulled pranks on them earlier in the week and maybe this was a very well done payback.

After a few minutes, I asked all of them to hit the showers and get ready for breakfast, with the exception of

Andy. After all, it was his Ouija board, so in the end, no matter who else might have been involved, he would have definitely had a hand in it—if this were in fact a prank.

Once the boys cleared out, I asked Andy to come clean and I would not say another word about it. He still played dumb, claiming he had no clue what I was talking about. I finally told him, point blank, "Andy, man, I found the Ouija board zipped up inside my pillowcase this morning. How the hell did it get there if you know nothing about it?"

As soon as I finished that sentence, Andy jumped up from his bed and grabbed the black duffle bag he had sitting on the top bunk. He quickly unzipped it and pulled out his Ouija board. The second I saw that thing, I almost passed out from becoming lightheaded so fast. I sat down on a neighboring bunk with my head in my hands. After a few moments, I told Andy to put it back in his bag and go join the rest of the boys.

I sat in their cabin for a solid ten minutes before getting up and walking out. I went straight to the Dumpster I had thrown the other Ouija board in earlier. I stopped myself a few feet from the Dumpster. Part of me wanted to jump in there and dig out the pieces; another part of me wanted to just forget about it and walk away.

After battling it out in my head, I decided to just let it be and walked away to meet up with the other counselors in the mess hall. Shortly after, breakfast was served and the entire camp went on to the planned daily activities. I never did look to see if the pieces of the Ouija board were still in the Dumpster.

The remainder of the week went without incident. I could tell every time I passed or spoke with Andy that he knew something had happened to me. I think he knew exactly what that was. Although we never talked about it again, I had the feeling he understood a lot more than he was letting on.

Andy graduated the following year, and to my knowledge he never mentioned what had happened to anybody. To this day, I have never seen nor spoken with him again. In fact, the last time I actually saw him was the final day of camp.

When I look back on that night and the following morning, I consider most of what happened to be easily dismissed as either coincidence or foolish games from high school students. But there were also some key elements in that experience that cannot be dismissed so easily. How did that board know when I had my first paranormal experience? What was that vibration I had felt through the planchette? Why did I fall ill and almost lose consciousness? *How the hell did that board get inside my pillowcase?*

Like I said, that was the first and last time I ever used a Ouija board. Many years have passed since I experienced this phenomenon and even today I cannot conclude what really happened. I am just not sure. If it was an elaborate prank pulled by those boys, they accomplished what most can never do—they kept their cool and never spilled the truth.

I really want to believe that what I experienced was nothing more than a joke. But part of me will not allow that, because there is a strong possibility I was in fact talking with a spirit named Morgana who appeared to have sinister attentions.

Over the years, I have contemplated experimenting with a Ouija board again, just to see if I could recreate the events from thirteen years ago. Although I have investigated and researched many scary and dangerous cases during my years of paranormal research, I cannot seem to find the will to pull out one of those boards again. If and when I eventually do, I plan to document the entire session with multiple video cameras, temperature gauges, electromagnetic field testers, and a few other pieces of equipment. Until then, I will always wonder about that night.

3 OLD CONEY CEMETERY

A night spent in the historic Old Coney Cemetery was my first official paranormal investigation. I was nineteen at the time and decided I would investigate the reports of ghost sightings in the cemetery. I was anxious to conduct some fieldwork and this seemed like the perfect place to start. I was eager to see if there was any truth to the long list of claims.

I had heard stories for years about a teenager buried there who had been killed in an automobile accident in the 1980s. There were many variations of the local ghost tale, repeated by both adults and teenagers, but one thing they all had in common was the legend that the ghost would kill anyone who came looking for him. The story also says that he was looking for a body to replace the one in his grave, so he could leave the cemetery. Allegedly, this trapped soul was unable to step foot off the cemetery grounds.

Old Coney Cemetery is located in my hometown of Lonaconing, Maryland. There are graves on the grounds dating back to the mid-1700s and maybe even earlier, long before the area became an official cemetery. It is located less than a mile off Route 36. The surrounding area in general has a rich history and there are a few historic houses within walking distance of the cemetery.

It was fall of that year, and I waited until about six in the evening before heading to the location. I was running rather primitive equipment compared to where I am presently with paranormal research. A few flashlights, rope, a thermometer, a compass, a knife, a notebook and pencil, a rabbit's foot, and a canteen full of water were about all I had. I used a military-issue backpack that I'd purchased at a local gun show to carry around my supplies.

People ask me all the time about the rabbit's foot. I bought it at a school fundraiser in the fifth grade simply because I thought it was neat. I used it as the key chain for my house key. For some reason, any time something positive happened, I attributed it to having the rabbit's foot in my pocket. I am not really a superstitious person, but the rabbit's foot just seemed to stick. To this day, I have a rabbit's foot attached to the vest I wear during paranormal investigations.

I parked at the local elementary school; from there, the cemetery was less than a mile away. The sun was slowly on its way to welcoming the moon so I needed to move fast. I wanted to have some daylight left upon arrival to make it easier in locating the gravesite. I threw my backpack on and started the uphill climb to the cemetery. A side road led right to the gates, so even though it was all uphill, the walk was easy and enjoyable.

I arrived at the entrance to the cemetery somewhere in the neighborhood of 6:45. Dusk had fully set in, but I located the grave in just a few minutes. The tombstone stood about three feet high and had the face of Mother Mary carved into the stone. The burial site was completely surrounded by a gated iron fence.

I entered through the gate and placed my backpack on the ground. I took out the notebook and ripped a sheet of paper out of it. I placed the sheet of paper directly onto the gravestone and rubbed my pencil back and forth until the entire contents of the stone had been transferred to the sheet of paper.

Gravestone-rubbing is a fairly easy way to transfer the detail from the headstone for documentation purposes and later research. The rubbing was something I could keep not only as a souvenir of sorts, but also as a quick reference when digging up facts about the deceased (pun intended). Today, that is achieved with a simple click on a cell phone camera.

After tucking away the gravestone rubbing into my backpack, I took out the thermometer and stuck it directly into the soil in the center of the burial site. I gave it a few minutes before logging in my notebook the temperature of the ground: sixty-seven degrees Fahrenheit. The temperature in the surrounding atmosphere was seventy-two degrees Fahrenheit. A five-degree difference did not seem like anything out of the ordinary, considering the cemetery sat in the shade of the surrounding woods. It made sense to me that the soil would be a little cooler.

The next thing I did was to place the compass on the soil of the burial site to monitor any significant magnetic changes that might occur. At this point, the night sky was fully dark so I had to use my flashlight to see the compass. The device worked perfectly and showed no sign of magnetic disturbance while I was monitoring it.

The time was now eight in the evening. The thermometer was now registering sixty-two degrees, which still was quite normal considering the sun had gone down. As I was sitting beside the burial site, the sound of rustling leaves from the back of the cemetery caught my attention. The wind was not blowing and it sounded as if something or someone was walking through the cemetery. I turned my flashlight off so I did not give away my location, if I had not already been seen by whoever it was.

I was not worried about trespassing, since the cemetery at that time did not have a curfew for visitors. The main gate was always open. However, I was worried about the intentions of this person walking around a cemetery in complete darkness. Of course, one would probably wonder the same thing of me, sitting by a grave with a thermometer stuck in the dirt.

What really aroused my suspicions was the fact that they had no visible light source. The cemetery was nearly pitch black and it would take nothing to trip over a grave. That is, assuming that the sound was coming from a person and not something else; most animals have excellent night vision.

I decided to get up off the ground and go investigate for myself. With my flashlight still turned off, I walked as slowly and quietly as possible through the cemetery. I could have kicked myself because I left the gate to the gravesite open, and because of its loose hinges, it swung back and forth, making a noticeable creaking sound. That was creepy in itself.

I tripped a few times while searching for whatever was making the walking sound. One trip put me face down in the grass and I banged up my knee pretty badly. When I hit the ground, I screamed in pain from my knee hitting a stone. I attempted to muffle the scream but was unsuccessful.

At that point, the rustling in the leaves started to move faster, in the opposite direction from me. I had startled whoever or whatever it was. It did not sound like an animal; in fact, it sounded just like I did when I walked through the cemetery. I was convinced it was a person.

I picked myself up from the ground and started walking back toward the grave I was originally sitting at. I was a little disoriented and could not immediately find my way back. Standing still for a moment, I just listened to the sounds around me and tried to allow my eyes to focus on the darkness a little better. Then, without warning, from across the cemetery, I heard a female voice sternly say, "Get out of here."

I could not tell if the voice was coming from an actual human being or something else. Regardless, somebody or something wanted me to vacate the premises. I kept staring in the direction the voice came from. My eyes widened in amazement as I started to see a glowing blue light appear about sixty feet in front of me.

At first, I thought it was just a flashlight, and that would explain the voice I'd heard moments earlier. I quickly ruled that out, however, since the light was growing ever so slightly without the sound of somebody walking toward me.

I decided to brave it and started slowly walking toward the blue glow. As I drew closer, I realized it was coming from the deceased teenager's gravesite. I was now about six feet from it. The light was bright, yet did not blind me or hurt my eyes. I took a few steps closer and noticed that the entire gravestone was surrounded by a blue, transparent sphere.

The carving of Mother Mary on the headstone was right in the center of the glowing circle of light, with her face being the brightest part. I am not much of a religious person, nor am I insinuating that this was some sort of divine visitation, but the overall characteristics of this occurrence were almost angelic.

I was now standing at the gate to the gravesite. All I wanted to do was pack up my belongings and respectfully leave. As I started to enter the area, my attention was quickly grabbed by someone or something coming out from behind the headstone. I can still see this image as clear as day in my head.

A woman, white as can be from head to waist, was peering from behind the gravestone and looking right at me. Her right hand held onto the side of the gravestone. It appeared as if she was wearing a robe with a hood. She was glowing as well, but not quite as much as the blue light I had seen before, surrounding the grave.

I stood paralyzed as we stared at one another. A wave of thoughts was racing through my head. Who is this woman? How is she connected to the dead teenager? What is she doing here? Why is she looking at me? Was it she who told me to leave?

I was staring face-to-face with a ghost.

I broke free from the spell I was under and started to reach down to grab my backpack. At that moment she started to walk around the gravestone. I panicked instantly by quickly lifting up my pack and running out of the cemetery, tripping and falling to the ground a few times on the way.

It seems funny to me when I look back on my first night of work in the paranormal field. That night I was a "run away from it" guy, and now I am a "run right at it" guy. It is amazing how a person can change over the years.

I was basically jumping down the road from running so fast. I looked back quickly a few times but the woman was nowhere in sight. I arrived back at my vehicle completely out of breath. I jumped into the car and just sat there in silence for a few minutes. I wanted to go back up there, yet I did not want to go back up there.

As I was battling myself over whether or not to go back, I realized I had left my compass and thermometer at the gravesite. The compass meant a great deal to me. It had been a gift from my grandfather, years prior. It was an original Boy Scouts of America compass made in 1936. There was no question about it—I had to get it back.

I started the car and placed my hands on the wheel, staring out at the road. I finally just said, "Screw it," and started driving back up Old Coney Cemetery Road. I arrived at the front gates and flipped on my high beams to light up the entire area. There was no one in sight.

I turned the headlights off and noticed that the mysterious blue light was no longer there. I talked myself into entering the cemetery again to gather up my belongings. Before doing so, I turned on the headlights once more, so everything was well lit. I left my door open and the vehicle running in preparation for a quick getaway, if necessary.

I did not run, but I did not stroll, either. I walked at a fast pace toward the grave, took a quick look around, and grabbed my compass and thermometer. To my surprise, the glass on the compass was completely shattered, rendering it inoperable, and the thermometer no longer worked properly either. It was stuck on thirty-one degrees Fahrenheit.

I jumped back into my car and headed home to contemplate my experiences from that evening. I do believe the atmosphere surrounding that gravesite bordered on paranormal, but I honestly cannot say that what I saw was a ghost. There may have been a scientific explanation for the blue light, perhaps some sort of chemical reaction involving natural gases.

The thermometer had me stumped as well. I could not think of anything in the area that would have caused the mercury inside the thermometer to freeze and stay in one spot. Mercury will not freeze easily and the temperature would have to be in the negative for that to even be possible. Even a thermometer containing nitrogen would have to be exposed to radical temperature changes to become trapped and stuck in the column.

The damaged compass was another baffling part of this case. Just like the thermometer, it would have taken extreme fluctuations in the temperature to have cracked that glass. The compass has since been repaired and restored to its original state. It is now locked up tight inside my father's safe.

I learned a great deal from my first night out on a paranormal case. I discovered a few unexplainable occurrences that could lead one to believe something supernatural was present in the cemetery. However, a female was never mentioned in any version of this local tale. Why a female dressed in a white robe was hiding behind a dead teenager's grave is beyond me. Maybe her ghost and her sighting were entirely unrelated to the case.

In 2011, fourteen years later, I returned to Old Coney Cemetery. It was nice to step foot on the grounds again. I felt comfortable. The location had changed somewhat. Many of the headstones were showing severe signs of deterioration. Much of the vegetation had been cut back or removed altogether. The original sign was gone; in fact, the cemetery remains unmarked. I found myself extremely disheartened by the neglect.

I absorbed the atmosphere for about an hour and then bid goodbye to the location that had started my journey into the realm of the unknown.

4 THE INDUSTRIAL FACILITY

The year 2007 delivered a landmark case for me. Not only was it the first time I worked with another paranormal researcher, but it was also the first time I documented paranormal activity on video. It is not every day that one films the ghost of a cowboy! This was also the first time I spent more than a week straight in one particular location. I was familiar with the town, having conducted research at various locations there in the past.

Per a recommendation from one of my clients, I was contacted by one of the employees of an industrial facility, who claimed to have seen an entity on numerous occasions. Other employees also had stories and claims of seeing a tall, dark, all-black figure roaming around the property. However, what initially brought me into this case was an interesting piece of video that the surveillance system had captured.

The night that the facility's surveillance caught the initial footage, an employee claimed to have been brushed aside, as if someone had walked past him, yet no one was there. Moments later, in an office area adjacent to where his experience occurred, the security camera caught an unexplainable anomaly. In the original surveillance clip, the camera was trained on a doorway in an office area. What was captured on video appeared to be a completely transparent, smoke-like entity flying through the doorway and across the office area. To describe it any better while making an assumption, I would say it appeared to be in a manifesting state.

I examined that footage for a solid month before agreeing to look into the claims. I could not come to any logical conclusion as to how this could be dismissed as something *not* paranormal. In order for me to come to any solid conclusion, I first needed to examine the area in which the video was taken.

The building itself is unusual. There are three levels to the place and the structure is a tiered, steel-beam design. In other words, the second floor is smaller than the first and the third floor is smaller than the second. The steel-beam construction forms a pyramid or triangle, yet the outside of the structure does not reflect that; from the outside it looks square. The housing of the triangular frame is all stone.

Another unique quality is that the building has no foundation. The first floor is literally open ground, or dirt, for lack of a better word. In the sales and electrical areas, a concrete slab was poured, but the bulk of the building lacks that. Each floor also has passageways behind the walls that connect and span the entire length of each floor, all the way around. This building is one of a kind.

Upon arrival, I started by interviewing a few employees to hear firsthand their claims of what they had dubbed the shadow man. All of their testimonies were tightly woven and nothing any of them said contradicted the others.

One of the employees spoke of a night he was shutting down the facility alone. He said he heard a man talking from another room, even though he was the only one present. He decided to investigate and walked through the door into the room where he heard the mysterious voice. It was dark and apparently empty. He claims that a cold chill came over him and he felt he was not the only one in that room. Hanging from the ceiling, just above a door, was the mandatory emergency exit sign. His eyes were focused on the lighted sign when it went completely black. He described it as being like when somebody walks past a light and for a brief moment the light is blocked. The hairs on the back of his neck stood straight up and he exited the building promptly.

A second employee spoke of his experience when he was on the second floor of the building, alone. Out of the corner of his eye, he could see a man standing to his left, about twenty feet away. He quickly jerked his head to get a better look, but the mysterious figure was gone. He ran over to the spot and no one was there. He quickly called one of the other employees, who confirmed that he was the only one on the second floor at the time.

The third employee I interviewed was authentically terrified, and refused to go anywhere in the building alone. He claimed that on numerous occasions somebody would whisper into his ear. Although the voice was right next to him, he could never make out the words being said. He said that on one night in particular, he kept spinning himself around quickly, certain that somebody was walking behind him, yet no one was ever there. He would hear footsteps following behind him, and even soft murmuring. The experience that rattled his senses was the time he was on the third floor and claims to have seen the shadow man just standing there, looking back at him. Then, without warning, the apparition was gone.

None of the employees inferred anything violent from this alleged entity. They all said that electrical malfunctions, doors opening and closing, and extreme temperature changes were the norm in his presence. The employees also noted that many times objects were found in areas different from where they had been left. They told me that the entity is most active during the winter months, but occasionally comes around in the summer. It was August when I talked to them.

This was one of the biggest investigations I had ever tackled. I was not fully prepared to cover such a large amount of space in just one night, let alone have the amount of equipment I would need to do so. One thing in my favor was the camera surveillance of the facility. It covered the majority of the building, with the exception of those passageways behind the walls, the restrooms, and the electrical room. So I figured I would just use handheld camcorders in any area outside of the surveillance grid. If there were anything within the surveillance grid that was relevant to the case, I would simply refer to that system to review it. Knowing full well that one night was not going to be enough time to fully research this place, and since the facility was currently inoperable, I requested a week.

It was also at this point when I realized that recruiting a full paranormal investigation team to accompany me on larger-scale cases would be necessary. Up until then, I had conducted my work alone. I always liked the idea of working alone. There was an intimacy to it. There was never the possibility of contamination of evidence by other people if no one else was in the building with me. So I never had a desire to start a team. However, since the research was the priority and I knew this case required more than I could offer, I decided to start one.

I contacted the one and only person I had in mind to start a team with: my best friend Bryan, who at that time had a fascination with cryptozoology. Even though cryptozoology had nothing to do with this case, Brian was also interested in the paranormal, and like me, had had paranormal experiences at a young age. I sent him all of the information I had at the time on the case and he gladly accepted.

Some brainstorming and quick wordplay gave birth to the P.I.T. Crew, short for Paranormal Investigation Team. This would mark the beginning of the direction my involvement in paranormal research would take. I figured having other individuals with me during investigations would add to the productivity and validity of potential findings. So the team began with just Bryan and me.

We arrived at eleven o'clock for the first night of research, focusing mainly on the office and stairwell where activity allegedly occurred. At the time, I was running laptop-based digital video recorders, which I placed in key areas throughout the building. I also placed audio recorders in the areas where voices had been heard. I personally carried film cameras, both video and still-shot. The first official night of research was really all about getting to know the facility's quirks and nuances. There was a lot of just sitting in one spot and listening, versus scouting around.

At two o'clock in the morning, I was stationed in the stairwell that connected the first and second floors of the building. Bryan was stationed in the office area where the original surveillance clip of an alleged apparition was caught. There was one camera trained on me, and another trained on Bryan. We kept in contact by means of two-way radios.

At 2:45, some activity began to present itself. Still sitting in the stairwell between the first and second floor, I began to hear what could only be described as footsteps coming from the next set of stairs above me. I listened for a few minutes before calling Bryan on the radio to verify he was still in the office area. He responded that he was still where he was supposed to be. After about ten minutes, the footsteps stopped. I called Bryan once more and asked him to come join me. I was about to go investigate the situation.

Bryan arrived at my location and we both proceeded to the third-floor stairwell to investigate the possible causes of the phantom footsteps. When we opened the door of the stairwell, a creepy hissing sound made us both jump back quickly. Unfortunately this was nothing paranormal. The hydraulic on the door was in need of oil and made a hissing sound when you opened or closed it.

We spent about an hour sitting in that area. The footsteps never returned and we were unable to recreate them by any logical means, excluding the possibility of another human being walking up there.

The rest of the first night produced no results. We left that morning with only the footsteps documented on the audio of my video camera. But we did capture them, so I left with a feeling of accomplishment. We went straight back to the office to review the cameras and audio recorders left in the areas we did not investigate. Nothing of significance was captured.

The second and third nights at the facility are barely worth mentioning. We had no personal experiences, nor did any of our equipment capture anything out of the ordinary. At this point, I was beginning to question the claims of the employees. But we still had four more nights of research to conduct, so there was still a chance that this activity could be documented.

The fourth night was a milestone in the investigation. We arrived there at the same time we did every evening, around 11:30. We stationed the cameras and audio recorders in the same areas as the previous three nights. But this time we felt it necessary to scout around the building with camcorders in hand. I hoped that this might stir up some activity, versus us just sitting in the same spots for hours on end.

We decided to start on the third floor and work our way down. At about one o'clock, we found a spot to sit and monitor the main area of the third floor. Bryan and I were talking, stationed behind a laptop recording video, when a strange object appeared close to the back wall across the room. It had a very inorganic appearance, and the way it moved was also abnormal.

Directly in front of us, we could not see anything, yet on the laptop screen we could clearly see something flying back and forth quickly in front of the camera. This object was not directly in front of the camera, though, since we could easily see a few feet in front of us.

The object appeared to change color ever so slightly every time it went past the camera's view. At one point, Bryan suggested an insect might be the culprit, but we soon agreed that it was not. The strange visual anomaly lasted approximately thirty seconds. After that, nothing else of relevance occurred on the third floor.

Following this occurrence, Bryan noticed a wooden panel on the wall of the third floor that stood out compared to the rest of the wall. There we discovered an entrance to the passageways that go back behind the walls of the facility, which I had been told about previously. We removed the panel and stepped briefly inside the passageway. After taking a quick look around, we agreed that an entire night needed to be dedicated to researching behind the walls. So we sealed the entrance back up.

Calling it a night, we once again packed up everything and headed back to the office to take a closer look at the third-floor anomaly. We examined the video capture for a few hours before deciding to review the audio recorders that were running the entire night. Lo and behold, one of the audio recorders had captured a vivid and clear disembodied voice. This particular audio recorder was left in the private bathroom of the first-floor office area. The voice on the recording can best be described as sounding like someone who had smoked cigarettes for fifty years, with a very gruff and low tone. It spoke the same phrase twice. The first time the phrase was spoken, it almost sounded like the speaker was right next to the recorder. The second time, it sounded farther away, as if the speaker were walking past the recorder and then away from it.

According to the time log on the recorder, the voice was captured at 5:37 in the morning. It had been recorded as we were gathering up the cameras and audio recorders throughout the building. That particular audio recorder was the last piece of equipment to be gathered up. You can hear me walking toward it and picking it up just moments before I turned it off. I picked up the audio recorder at 5:49, just twelve minutes after this voice had been captured. The unsettling part about this audible capture was what had been said. The voice on the recorder said two words: "Don't go."

Bryan and I sat in awe, amazed at such a clear and potentially significant capture. It is all speculation, of course, but it was as if this entity knew we were packing up to leave. The productivity of the case went up a notch at that point. We walked away from the fourth night of research with a strange visual anomaly captured on the third floor and a very distinct voice captured on the first floor.

The fifth night we decided to dedicate to the passageways behind the walls of the building. We dubbed these areas *corridors*. We started off through the entrance discovered on the third floor the previous night. With just a single camcorder and two flashlights, we were running rather primitive. We did not want to weigh ourselves down with much equipment, since it was unclear what exactly was behind these walls.

We scoured the third-floor corridors for about two hours, from 11:30 in the evening to about 1:30 in the morning. In certain areas, the third-floor corridors had six-foot-diameter holes in the floor, so we had to be very careful where we stepped. Through the holes we could also see the second-floor corridors. There was no way to get to the second-floor corridors from the third floor, aside from dropping down one of those holes. However, the drop was approximately fifty feet.

I decided to search for a way to enter the second-floor corridors. We left that area and headed down to the second floor. It took about twenty minutes to find a way into the second-floor corridors. This time it was through an actual wooden door, as opposed to the wooden wall panel on the third floor.

At two o'clock, we entered the second-floor corridors. Within just moments, the door we came through slammed shut. That caught our attention, to say the least, so we started to examine the door itself. It was basically a piece of plywood with two-by-fours acting as the framework on both sides. Two three-inch hinges attached the door to the frame within the wall. A fairly simple design, but it worked. We opened and closed the door a few times, examining it for anything that could cause it to shut abruptly like it had moments earlier. Nothing out of the ordinary stood out as being the cause.

As Bryan and I were walking away, the door slowly started to open back up, creating a creepy and clichéd creaking sound. Once again, this caught our attention and we went back to examine the door. There was no breeze or air current flowing from either direction. The corridors were not temperature-controlled in any way and we logged temperatures over ninety degrees.

Normally, when a door shows activity such as this, it is easily proven to be due to some form of air current. This door would not only open on its own, but it would also close on its own. Nothing could explain how this door could seemingly open and close by itself. Logically, an air current would have to be coming from both directions, inside and outside the door at different times, to make it do that. Either that, or someone or something was pushing and pulling it.

Considering all of the research time we had spent on the second floor over the past few days, we would have seen or heard a creaky wooden door opening and closing. This activity seemed to have started once we entered that area.

The door opened and closed various times right in front of us over the next thirty minutes. Unable to come to a logical conclusion as to why it was happening, we left the door open and decided to explore the rest of the second-floor corridors.

We roamed around for about an hour with nothing of significance occurring. It was now 3:30. As we were heading back toward the door we came through, the lights in the corridors suddenly came on. I hadn't even noticed that there were lights in there to begin with.

The lights were single bulbs along the wall, about twenty feet apart from one another. Now that they were on, I could see a light switch to the left of the door, and the switch was in the up position. I instructed Bryan to turn the lights back off. He did so and took a few steps back away from the door, which was open. He was now standing about four feet from it. I was about ten feet from him, documenting with the camcorder.

We stood there in silence for a few moments. Then Bryan took a step toward the door and it slammed shut right in front of him. I instructed him to open it back up. He said that he felt whatever was there did not want us to leave. No sooner did he say that, the door closed again on its own, as if responding to his assertion.

While this was going on, I noticed another hallway branching off from the corridor we were in. We decided to explore that hallway, and Bryan opened the door once more. We started walking away when I told him I felt like the door was reacting to the things we had been saying. As soon as I said that, the door slammed shut.

After another episode watching the door, we finally decided to venture down that other hallway. I set the camcorder down and left it recording. I aimed it down the hallway we were about to explore. The camera could also see the corner of the wall the door was on.

We eventually walked so far down the hallway into the darkness that the camera could no longer see us. After spending about twenty minutes exploring this other area, we started heading back to where the camera was left recording. We later discovered it caught the door opening once more while we were gone.

As we approached the camera, the door slammed shut one last time. With the angle the camera was at, we could see the shadow of the door opening while we were out of view and then closing as we returned.

At four o'clock in the morning, we left the corridors and started packing up our gear for the night. Upon arriving back at the office, we immediately started reviewing the video footage from the corridor investigation. Watching it verified that the door had opened once more after we left the camera's view, and it also verified it closing for the final time.

The activity with the door was a mystery that could not be solved by logical means. Five nights into the research of the facility had produced some credible evidence of the paranormal activity claimed to be present there. But it still wasn't enough to completely seal the deal for me.

On the sixth night, I decided to focus on the electrical room of the facility. The electromagnetic fields in that room were through the roof, and I felt that out of all the areas in the building, this would be the one to generate some significant activity. It is believed that apparitions— or spirits, or entities, or whatever you want to call them— require some form of energy to manifest, communicate, or move things. It just made sense to me that the one room that powered the entire building would be the most likely to offer up such a situation. I was right.

We stationed ourselves in the electrical room of the building. Two laptops armed with digital video recorders were running, as well as two camcorders. We sat monitoring the video surveillance for about three hours, until 2:30 in the morning.

Looking at one of the laptop screens, Bryan pointed out that something was slightly moving toward the back of the room, directly underneath the electrical panels, near the floor. At first I was unable to see what he was talking about. I was looking at the back of the room and also looking at the surveillance monitor.

After a few moments, I did see what he was talking about. The anomaly was faint and moved in a subtle fashion. If we both had not seen it, I would have dismissed it as my eyes playing tricks on me. In the beginning stages, it appeared white and transparent and looked like a two-foot-wide span of smoke lying on the floor. Then it moved again, and its appearance became more vivid to both of us. I was literally questioning this occurrence out loud to Bryan, with less than gentlemanly words. After a few minutes it vanished entirely. We both felt it had gone and was finished doing whatever it was doing.

Then, without warning, the same thing flew down from the ceiling in a swooping fashion and landed on the floor. Both of us were totally amazed. The second sighting gave more depth to its appearance. It still had a white, smoke-like appearance, yet this time it exhibited a more plasma-like exterior that almost seemed electrical in nature. It was like an oblong concentration of energy about three feet long.

This anomaly stayed on the floor for a few minutes before rising up to the left and falling back down. Then it once again vanished. This was one of the strangest occurrences I had ever seen and it was right in front of me. Whatever it was had no scientific explanation that I know of.

We called it a night earlier than we had the previous nights. Something extraordinary had been captured on our cameras and we did not want to wait another minute to extensively review it. About 3:15, we packed it all up and headed back to the office for another session of reviewing the material.

The seventh night of research came and went and produced nothing paranormal. That was a little disappointing for me, considering that the evidence we had already gathered throughout the week looked promising. I requested one more night of research and unfortunately was turned down. The facility was due to open back up for operation, running twenty-four hours a day. Technically we had researched the place for eight nights already, if you count the night of interviewing the employees and scouting out the place. But I just wasn't satisfied. We were so close. The place showed so much promise and had produced some well-documented activity.

I asked for permission to leave cameras running in the electrical room of the building for twenty-four-hour surveillance. This was the one room that had produced the most compelling footage so far, and it was also the only room that did not have in-house surveillance. The owners obliged, as long as they would not be held responsible for any damage that might occur to our equipment.

Since I had to leave the surveillance running for twenty-four hours, there was no way I could use camcorders for this. So I stationed a laptop in the electrical room, rigged with cameras to record all activity on the hard drive. I also ran a video camera into a twenty-four-hour videocassette recorder, so there was no compromise in recording with both film and digital means.

I was permitted to enter the building early each morning to transfer all of the footage from the laptop to another laptop and commence recording again. I also removed the videocassette and replaced it with a blank one each day.

For four months, I stopped in each morning to transfer the footage and start recording again. I was determined to capture more of this activity. I would occasionally speak with the employees in hopes of hearing about new encounters. There was never anything new to report on their end.

One day in early December proved that determination and constant research of an allegedly active location is a must in this field. I retrieved the footage and took it back to the office as usual. As I was waiting for Bryan to arrive and help, I started reviewing it myself. Within an hour of scanning through the video surveillance, I spotted something shooting across the screen. Since it happened so fast, it took me a moment to locate that exact section again in the footage. Once I did, I played it back about six times slower than normal speed.

I could not believe what I was seeing. That could have been it. That could have been him. That could very well have been the shadow man the employees were so adamant about seeing. I quickly marked the beginning and end of the clip and saved it as a separate file. I must have watched it two hundred times before realizing I should have called Bryan.

I rang Bryan's phone and the first words out of my mouth were, "You are never going to believe this!" Of course, with an opening like that, he was curious as can be. I told him that we had possibly caught the shadow man and he needed to come see for himself. I could tell he was in disbelief, yet at the same time quietly excited.

Bryan arrived and I showed him the footage. The shadow man had a few very distinctive characteristics, one of which is what appeared to be a fedora or cowboy hat. In the video clip, he quickly walks from the left of the room to the right. Although it's speculation, I also get the feeling he was looking directly at the camera. It was almost like he knew it was there. Bryan pointed out something I had not noticed—a faint red glow coming from the apparition. We agreed that it also appeared as if he were carrying something in his left hand.

We quickly packed up the laptop and headed back to the industrial facility to show the employees the footage. Up until this point, we had not revealed a single piece of evidence to them. I am very particular about what I call paranormal and even more particular about what I show a client as being paranormal. In most cases, before I present anything, I make the clients aware that they need to come to their own conclusions based on the evidence they are about to see and hear.

Luckily for us, the three original employees I had interviewed months ago for the case were working on site. I waited until their lunch break and we all sat down in the employee break room. Before playing the file, I warned them that this footage had not been validated and that there was always the possibility of video interference playing a role. Considering this was captured on digital equipment and they were seeing it only hours after I discovered it, I needed to leave room for a possible valid explanation to be found. Then I hit play.

I have to admit that a feeling of demented joy overcame me when I saw all three of the employees widen their eyes during the viewing. As the shadow man came across the screen, I witnessed the hair on six arms stand straight up alongside thousands of goosebumps. All three of them just sat there in silence, watching.

I had the video clip looping, so every few seconds the shadow man would appear on the screen. After about three minutes of this, one of the employees said that was enough. I asked the three of them what they thought about it and they all said it was in fact what they had been seeing all this time. My research was complete for the time being.

The industrial facility was one of the most productive investigations I had ever conducted. It took eight nights and four months of monitoring to gather the data I did. I have always believed that in order to experience what a client is experiencing, you must become the client yourself. That is not always possible in every situation, but in many cases I have been fortunate enough to spend a *lot* of time researching.

A few months later, the footage of this alleged apparition appeared on the NBC Universal program *Shocking... Scary... Paranormal Videos*. It was not long after the shadow man footage was released that viewers started to dub him "the cowboy."

5 POLTERGEIST

I can honestly say that up until early spring of 2008, I'd never worried that I would be in a situation where I'd be dodging flying objects. In my years of paranormal research, it has been a rarity to cross paths with anything violent in nature. Depending on how you look at it, I am either lucky or unlucky to have had minimal experiences with the darker side of the paranormal. So when I was approached with a poltergeist case that bordered on dangerous, I welcomed the experience.

The nature of poltergeist activity is known to most people, due in large part to a series of special effects-laden films that were popular in the early 1980s. Documented poltergeist activity dates back to the late 1600s. Over the years, there have been a few very well-documented cases by physicists and paranormal investigators. The most commonly reported poltergeist phenomena include random objects moving or floating through the air, light bulbs exploding, objects glowing white, objects bending or burning, televisions powering on and off, and unexplainable cracking and hammering sounds.

I have researched alleged poltergeist activity in the past. In most cases, I was able to dismiss the occurrences through scientific means and rational deduction. The clients I dealt with didn't have an extreme case where the spirit was a nuisance or repeat offender. In most cases, there were one or two unexplainable occurrences that sent them running in the direction of the poltergeist label.

Sometimes a simple event can cause the most dramatic effect. Something as simple as a loose floorboard, if stepped on just right, can send a vibration across a wooden floor, resulting in a piece of furniture shaking just enough to cause an object to fall from it. This was the case with one of my clients. She was relieved to know there was not anything paranormal occurring in her home.

Other cases produced similar results. I call it the ripple effect. One thing can easily lead to another and people misinterpret what they have experienced. Paranormal researchers have the luxury of looking for these clues after the fact. When clients experience something, they are simply going through their day-to-day routine and find themselves caught off-guard by something that does not normally happen. There is no time for rational thought in those situations. But when entering a client's home, I already know the symptoms; I simply need to find the cause. One case, however, did produce some shocking evidence in favor of poltergeist activity. The fieldwork I conducted at this location was both productive and unsettling.

I was approached by a family living in Longs, South Carolina, who allegedly were experiencing violent occurrences within their home. Their claims ranged from inanimate objects flying at them to electronic devices exploding. They reported to me that this activity occurred four to five times a week at different times of the day. The activity was unpredictable but always seemed to be harmful in nature. They had no clue as to why it was occurring and were unaware of any possible motive. The reported poltergeist activity did not happen throughout their entire house. It was restricted to their master bedroom and bathroom area. Not one time did this family experience anything outside of those two rooms.

I decided to accept the case and scheduled a night to conduct research in their home. I have a rule that I do not ever stray from: I do not allow any members of my paranormal team to accompany me on cases that could be potentially dangerous. Members of my team have children and families and I just could not live with something horrible happening to one of them, knowing that I could have prevented it. So I took this case alone.

Since the activity was sporadic, I planned to start in the afternoon and continue on throughout the night. I arrived at the residence at three in the afternoon. As I normally do, I did a full sweep of the home, logging baseline data from various pieces of equipment like the electromagnetic field tester and thermometer. I also stationed multiple surveillance cameras in the master bedroom and bathroom to document the entire investigation.

After about an hour of preparation, I decided to start focusing on the affected rooms. I started with the master bathroom. After two hours of uneventfully sitting and waiting, I relocated to the master bedroom. It was home to half a dozen porcelain dolls that added their own "creep factor" to the room. They just stared at me, completely lifeless, yet I felt like something was inside looking out. Needless to say, I was not a big fan of them.

It was about six in the evening now and I had yet to experience anything out of the ordinary. Staking out two rooms can become tedious when nothing is occurring. At seven o'clock, I decided to walk around the house as if I were living there. I thought maybe that was why I was not experiencing anything. The house was quiet and lifeless; the family was gone for the night.

I walked through the house, turning lights on and purposely creating noise to make my presence known. Nine in the evening rolled around and I had yet to document anything to validate or disprove the clients' claims. I returned to the master bedroom in hopes of stirring up some activity. I sat at the foot of the bed in silence for quite some time.

Then a sliding sound came from the dresser against the wall. This, of course, directed my attention to those creepy dolls, which were sitting on the dresser. I did not see anything move, but it did sound like something slid across the top of it. I glanced down at the EMF tester and noted the field was ten points higher than it had been when I conducted my initial sweep. Immediately after, I heard what could only be described as a thick scratching sound, coming down the wall to my right.

I stood up, trying in various ways to recreate the sound, and was eventually successful. I used my index finger and dragged it along the wall. That sound was close, but not exact. What I'd heard had more depth to it. So I dragged all five fingers across the wall. This recreated the sound almost perfectly. I believed something had scratched the wall, only I could not see what that something was.

I was now standing directly in front of the dresser. There was a tall lamp to my left. I noticed the EMF tester was registering five points higher than earlier. It was now sitting at a solid 0.16 on the Tesla scale (Tesla is a unit of measurement for magnetic fields). As I moved the tester closer to the wall where I heard the scratching sound, the number gradually increased. I had the meter close to the lamp when the light mysteriously turned on, right in front of me. At that moment, the EMF tester was registering 107. This was incredible. I had to unplug the lamp to get it to turn off; turning the switch did not affect it. I plugged the lamp back in and it worked fine when I switched it off and on, so it was not a faulty switch.

I stood there in silence for a few moments. Then I noticed the closet door was vibrating every so often, very lightly. It was vibrating enough to cause the doorknob to make a rattling sound. I looked around for an explanation. There was not a central air vent nearby to cause enough air movement to move the door.

The door suddenly stopped vibrating and I could hear movement coming from inside the closet. I opened the closet door and looked for air vents inside. There were none to be found. I could still hear something moving toward the back of the closet. I shined my flashlight there and saw a leather jacket swinging on the rack.

I stood still, watching it sway back and forth. I slowly approached the rack with my EMF tester. It is extremely rare to see this tester actually add an additional decimal point to the readout. Underneath the jacket, the EMF was so high that the meter registered two decimal points. I had only seen this a few times throughout the years. A field that high was uncanny for a private residence. There were no major power lines outside of the home or nearby radio towers to justify such a high reading.

One thing the clients forgot to tell me was that they had witnessed a woman's purse floating in midair in that closet at one point. After the investigation, when I reported my findings, they remembered to tell me about that.

Once the activity in the closet subsided, I decided to venture up into the attic to explore the possibility of faulty electrical work being the cause of the high EMFs. The attic was airtight and the electrical work appeared to be up to par. In fact, the highest number I registered on the EMF tester up there was 0.04. I left the attic to return to the master bedroom.

As I approached the room, I could hear a loud static sound coming from inside. Also, although I had left the door open, when I returned it was closed. I cautiously opened it to discover a clock radio on a nightstand had been turned on. The needle on the tuner was in between two clear channels, transmitting nothing but white noise and random radio broadcasts cutting in and out.

Alarm clocks are infamous for giving off high electromagnetic fields, so I did not look too much into the 0.40 it was registering. Just like the lamp, the radio had not physically been turned on. The switch was still in the off position. I unplugged it to get it to stop and the room was quiet once more.

It was now midnight, and I stood at the side of the bed, waiting for the next wave of activity to occur. I had yet to witness the reported flying objects, although I had experienced everything else the clients mentioned. I could not come to a rational explanation as to how these occurrences were happening.

The next thing that happened still sends shivers down my spine. Up until then, I had never been physically attacked in any way by an entity during my research. I was still standing beside the bed when I heard something moving, either in or around the dresser with the porcelain dolls. Once again I found myself staring at them. I started walking toward the dresser very slowly. The closer I got, the more I started to think that maybe a mouse was behind the dresser or even in one of the drawers. That also could have explained the sounds I heard earlier. I stopped about three feet from the dresser. The sound stopped as well.

The room was completely silent. I stood there listening and listening, yet all I could hear was the quietness of the room. Then, without warning, a spool of thread flew from the top of the dresser and hit me directly in my right eye. After it hit, instead of bouncing backwards upon impact, it went *around* me and fell to the ground.

Now, I am no physicist, but I am well aware of the common laws of gravity and impact. That spool of thread should have either fallen to the ground in front of me, or bounced off me, back in the direction from which it came. It did no such thing. It struck me and then literally went behind me before hitting the floor. I turned around and spotted the spool of thread on the floor. I bent over to pick it up and was startled by the alarm clock turning back on to pure white noise once again.

I grabbed the alarm clock, remembering I had unplugged it previously. I noted that the plug was still out of the socket. It was somehow functioning without conventional power. I threw it on the bed and the sound stopped.

I ran over to one of the stationary surveillance cameras I had set up. I put my face close to the lens and pointed to my eye. The video clearly documents my right eye showing signs of having been struck. It was puffy and red, and when compared to the other, the difference was undeniable. Although I wasn't pleased by the attack, I was pleased that this same surveillance camera had captured it.

I returned to the spot beside the bed where the attack had taken place. I scoured the entire area in search of that spool of thread. I was unable to locate it. Immediately after the incident, I had turned around and seen it lying on the floor. At some point, between my walking over to the camera and documenting my injury and returning to that spot, the spool had moved again.

The damage to my eye put me in a position I do not like to be in: I had to end the investigation prematurely. I have another rule: paranormal research starts with the researchers and investigators themselves, and if they are not physically and mentally capable of conducting research to the best of their ability, they are a hindrance to the productivity of the case. I had been hurt. The vision in my right eye was blurred. I could no longer rely on myself to report accurately what I might see.

I called the clients and informed them that I would be departing earlier than expected. I advised them to stay where they were for the evening, just to be safe. I could tell they were concerned, yet at the same time excited that I was able to witness what they had been experiencing.

What I witnessed and experienced certainly falls within the realm of poltergeist activity. There was something completely out of the ordinary happening in my clients' house. I documented nearly everything they had warned me about, and then some.

Many people are unaware there are actual scientific explanations for most poltergeist phenomena. The documented effects of electromagnetism are identical to what has been regarded as poltergeist or paranormal activity. Electromagnetism in the proper setting can make inanimate objects move, bend steel, create light anomalies, and even cause fires. Knowing this, my future research into this private residence will focus on the effects of electromagnetism. My clients may very well be experiencing authentic paranormal occurrences, but until I can rule out the possibility of electromagnetism playing a role, I cannot reach a definite conclusion. Either way, they are in a potentially dangerous situation.

Electromagnetism is to the paranormal field what gravity is to the Earth. Entities or spirits may be using electromagnetism deliberately, or they may not be using it at all. It may be something they are drawn to, or maybe they act as a magnet themselves. For now, we just don't know. But years from now, I believe that what most people now consider as paranormal will be considered a part of everyday life, thanks to ongoing scientific research.

6 · EMILY'S HOUSE

There is nothing more disheartening than dealing with the spirit of a child. As a father myself, I tend to prioritize cases revolving around children over anything else. Call me empathetic, I guess, but when I hear the story of a child who not only lost her own life but her entire family to a mysterious illness, it becomes extremely difficult not to feel saddened and regretful.

In October 2008, I was contacted by a woman I'll call Mrs. Linda, the owner of a historic building in Georgetown, South Carolina. She claimed that the ghosts of a little girl named Emily and Emily's father were still present, and had become a part of her family. She said that the little girl would tug on her pants leg quite often, as if asking to be picked up and held, among many other encounters with both spirits.

On one occasion, Mrs. Linda was having a dinner party at her apartment. Everybody was sitting around the dinner table, enjoying one another's company. One of her male guests started to look annoyed. He finally asked out loud if the person kicking his chair would quit doing that. Nobody at the table admitted to kicking his chair. At this point, Mrs. Linda started to tell her guests about the spirits in her home. They did not seem too enthused about her story, nor did they seem to believe her.

Mrs. Linda asked the spirits to show her guests that they were really there. The woman sitting to her right immediately jumped out of her chair, claiming something had just tugged on her dress. The man whose chair had been kicked was still in disbelief, claiming the woman was just spooked by their hostess's storytelling. At that point, a visible scratch slowly appeared on his arm. His eyes widened and he rolled up his sleeve to show everybody at the table. Every guest sat there and watched this mysterious scratch slowly grow in length down his arm, right before them. Of course, the hostess just smiled, with that "I told you so" look on her face.

When Mrs. Linda contacted me, she was seeking a reputable paranormal researcher to help her reach out to little Emily and hopefully aid in finding peace for the two spirits. She claimed that they speak to her on an almost daily basis. She said that the little girl is named Emily, and she believes the gentleman spirit to be Emily's father, since she has been told that many times by Emily herself. She has yet to find out his name. She has experienced hearing them walk around the apartment at night while talking to each other. She said she could tell the difference between the girl and the father through the way they chose to communicate and interact with the living.

Mrs. Linda's century-old, two-story building contains several businesses and apartments. The structure has had little renovation over the years. Inside, the original air shafts that older buildings used for ventilation, allowing air to flow in and out, are still present, although the majority have been sealed off. The floors are not level, causing a person to feel a sense of unbalance while walking around. The section of the building I was called to investigate was one of the second-floor apartments.

This apartment consisted of seven rooms that were obviously not originally designed to function as living quarters. The closets were made of the original stonework and also had the airshafts present. One of the closets in particular used to be a stairway that led to the roof, now sealed off and converted into a closet. I could still see the original stairs, only now they led to a newly finished ceiling.

There was not a single door in the apartment, other than the one at the bottom of the stairs that led up to it.

The rooms were very small, with the largest being about ten feet by ten feet. The ceilings were noticeably high, an astounding fifteen feet from the floor to the ceiling.

According to Mrs. Linda, in the early twentieth century a married couple and their daughter resided in the apartment. The couple had recently relocated from New York. A few weeks after they arrived in South Carolina, their nine-year-old daughter fell deathly ill. Local doctors could not come to any conclusions as to what was wrong with her. All that any professional could agree on was the fact that this young girl could not survive the illness.

Her mother left the city of Georgetown in search of a doctor who could cure her daughter's sickness before it was too late. The mother never returned, and nothing was ever found to explain her disappearance.

Not knowing that his wife would never return, the father had no choice but to leave his sick daughter alone in the apartment each day while he went to work. According to his journal, each day she appeared to sink deeper into this mysterious illness.

Every day his daughter would ask about her mother, wondering when she would come home. Weeks later, she was to the point in her illness where she could not even speak. The man's journal noted multiple times that his daughter would lie in bed with her arms out, as if asking for her mother to hold her.

Six weeks had passed since his wife left to search for help. His daughter had fallen into a completely unresponsive state and would stare at the ceiling for hours on end without even blinking. In the journal, he described her as being lifeless, yet alive. Soon he too fell ill and could no longer tend to his daughter's needs. His last journal entry mentioned finding "little Emily" dead and he was unclear for how long, since he had not been out of bed for days. It seemed to be his final thought.

There is nothing documented as to who eventually found their bodies or how long they had been dead in the apartment. According to records, the apartment remained empty for decades following their deaths. It is believed that potential renters were simply afraid of contracting the same unknown deadly illness that killed the little girl and her father.

With a backstory like that, I had to take the case to see for myself whether Emily was truly still in the apartment. Mrs. Linda certainly was adamant about it, and I knew she believed it, whether it was true or not. My interactions with her showed her to be a very spiritual lady with a heart of gold. I saw no signs of psychological issues, nor did I see any signs of story fabrication.

The building was no stranger to paranormal investigators. A few years prior, another paranormal investigation group had conducted research there, and turned up a pile of evidence in the form of disembodied vocalizations on audio recordings. The place showed promise.

I assembled a team of four investigators and we arrived in Georgetown at nine in the evening. We unloaded all of the gear and met briefly with Mrs. Linda. Then she left for the evening, and at about 10:30 we began our investigation into the alleged ghosts of Emily and her father.

Initially, we noted many bars and restaurants in the area, which people were going in and out of nearly the entire night. We considered this significant, since low voices were one of the claims from the client.

The living area of the apartment was extremely high in electromagnetic fields. They were consistent and abnormally high for a residential living area. Since there were no fluctuations in the readings, I dismissed the data as being caused by typical household electrical devices. However, on the flip side, the high EMFs could also be contributing to delusions and paranoia in the client, since being exposed to such a high field often causes such symptoms.

After conducting a full sweep of the building, I split the team up into pairs, placing two of my investigators in the dining area and myself with another investigator in the living area. I decided to conduct a communication session. With such high EMFs, the potential for an entity to communicate was also high. The two investigators in the dining area remained quiet during this time, so as not to contaminate my session. They continued to log temperature variations, electromagnetic fields, and even ion levels in their area.

Sitting in the living room with my partner, who I'll call Stanley, I placed an EMF tester on the arm of the couch we were sitting on. The meter displayed a steady seven in Gauss mode (Gauss is a unit of measurement for magnetic fields). That is quite high for an area the client often sits in for hours on end.

To my right was an end table with four books stacked on it, all related to spirituality and life after death. In front of us was a coffee table on which we had placed the audio recorders and a cell phone in hopes of capturing a voice or other activity. On the opposite side of the coffee table was a live five-foot-tall plant in a pot, covered with hundreds of tiny green leaves.

Having a daughter of my own, it was easy for me to relate to the little girl spirit that potentially was there. I started asking questions out loud and saying the typical things an adult would say to a child. I referred to our equipment as "toys" in a welcoming tone, hoping that she would come out to play with us.

Since the EMF tester was directly to my right on the arm of the couch, I decided to focus on that. It was still showing a consistent reading of seven. I asked Emily to come play with the "toy" on the arm of the couch. I told her that all she had to do was touch it and we would know she was there. A few minutes passed and the reading did not budge at all.

I started speaking of my own daughter and how we play together all the time. I told Emily that I believed she liked playing with her father, too. At that moment, the plant adjacent to where we were sitting started to move ever so slightly. The tiny leaves started falling to the ground as if somebody or something had brushed by it to approach the coffee table.

I kindly asked Emily whether she had just walked by the plant, and the EMF tester went up five points to a twelve before quickly returning to the baseline seven I had previously logged. So far, the occurrences could be dismissed as coincidental. So I asked Emily to come play with me. I asked her once again to touch the "toy" sitting on the arm of the couch. I reiterated that if she touched it, we would know she was there.

No sooner did I finish stating that when the EMF tester increased instantly from a seven to a seventeen. It jumped ten points in less than a second and then immediately returned to the baseline seven. It was almost as if she touched it quickly, in a timid fashion, and immediately backed off.

The maximum reading on the tester during this session hit twenty-one. Immediately afterward, the plant began to drop leaves once more. It seemed as if the spirit had walked away from us and gone back to hiding behind that plant.

I grabbed the EMF tester and started testing the levels in and around the plant. Behind it, the meter displayed a fourteen. It was obvious that there was nothing electrical in or around the plant to justify such a high reading. We were starting to believe that Emily was standing behind it. Stanley grabbed a temperature-reading device and started logging the room's temperature. In most of the room he logged a temperature of seventy-four degrees Fahrenheit. But when he placed the temperature gauge behind the plant, he logged a temperature of fifty-six degrees. There was an eighteen-degree difference between the back of the plant and the rest of the living room. This was during the winter months with no air conditioning running. There was no heat venting of any kind around this area, either. Then suddenly, the temperature gauge and the EMF tester reset to their previously logged baseline readings for the room. The little girl was gone.

I reported to the other investigators what we had experienced in the living area. From the numerous shifts in the electromagnetic fields, to the leaves from the plant falling on two different occasions, to the radical temperature difference between the plant and the room, I felt we had located something.

The time was now around midnight. I switched on the magnetic pickup attached to my vest in hopes of being able to hear any anomalies traveling throughout the room. Immediately, a very faint static field could be heard coming through the amplifier. As I waved the magnetic pickup throughout the room, the field amplified as I approached the doorway to the master bedroom.

All three investigators followed me into the bedroom as I tracked the audible magnetic field. Inside, the field jumped around sporadically, quickly moving from one side of the room to the other numerous times. Just when the field would strengthen in volume, it would dissipate and require being tracked again. This went on for at least twenty minutes. Back and forth across the bed the field would move as if someone or something that we could not see was jumping on and off of it. Stanley attempted to log EMFs with his meter, but the fields were moving too fast to get a solid reading.

The audible electromagnetic field fell silent. I was now at the head of the bed, while Stanley with the EMF tester was at the foot of it. A few moments after I lost the audible field, his meter started logging a seven where he was standing. I quickly moved toward the foot of the bed and the audible field became present again. While all of this tracking was going on, the other two investigators were taking photographs and monitoring the temperature of the room.

As Stanley and I continued to track the moving field across the room, this time it led us into the corner of the room closest to the door. The Gauss level increased on his EMF meter while my magnetic pickup amplified in volume. The field was getting stronger.

The amplifier hit such a volume that it caused an ear-piercing squeal, prompting me to shut it down. We were still monitoring the field through the EMF tester. Both of us were crammed into the corner of the room, waiting for something to happen. The tester was now holding steady at a twenty-two.

I risked another glass-shattering squeal from the magnetic pickup amplifier and turned it back on. The field was still very loud, but tolerable. As I moved the magnetic pickup through the air, we all froze in our tracks when a little girl's voice came out of the amplifier. I instantly asked if everyone present had heard it and of course they had. The voice said only one word: *Mommy.*

I was moved, to say the least. Was that little Emily speaking to us? Was it her that we had been chasing throughout the two rooms all night? The team was worked up and excited at what we had just heard. We went back into the living area to collect ourselves. The time was now one o'clock in the morning.

As we stood in the living room discussing the findings so far, we started to hear somebody coming up the stairs of the apartment. At first, we thought it was Mrs. Linda returning home to check on our progress. The footsteps stopped just shy of the landing where the entrance to the apartment was. I was still thinking it was the client; maybe she had stopped to listen quietly, so she did not disturb our research. After about a minute, I went to see if she were standing on the stairs. To my surprise, nobody was there.

The look on the team members' faces was priceless. We had all heard somebody walking up those steps. They were wooden, and when you walked on them, a distinctive, hollow, percussive sound would occur. Even with bare feet or wearing socks, the boards creaked something fierce. It would be nearly impossible for any person to come up or go down those stairs without being detected.

The team confirmed that nobody was standing on the stairs. The door at the bottom of the staircase was still locked. There was no apartment above us or even another staircase that could have caused that sound.

We spent another two hours researching the apartment, with little result. The phantom footsteps seemed to have been the last of the activity for that evening. At three o'clock, I decided to call it a night and we began packing up the gear.

I called Mrs. Linda and she promptly returned. I gave her my initial impression of our findings and she was quite pleased with the results. The team and I finished loading the gear back into our vehicles and we hit the road to head home.

When I consider the sad history of the place—the unpleasant deaths of both Emily and her father and the mysterious disappearance of her mother—it is difficult to dismiss the possibility of them still being present in that apartment. I cannot help but think that little Emily may still be searching for her mother.

According to her father's journal, all Emily wanted was for her mother to hold and comfort her. Those phantom footsteps coming up the stairs to the apartment could have been her father returning home from work, just as he did one hundred years ago. That part is speculation, but I do have to keep the history of the place in mind. The investigation produced some odd occurrences and experiences, and that voice saying *Mommy* still haunts me today.

7 POOGAN'S PORCH

I have to tell you right off the bat that what sparked my interest in Poogan's Porch restaurant was the Travel Channel deeming it as the third most haunted location in America—along with the existence of police reports documenting elusive trespassers. It really says something when the police get involved with a ghost! With a reputation like that, I just had to experience it for myself.

Poogan's Porch is located in historic Charleston, South Carolina. The restaurant opened in 1976 and was named after Poogan, a stray dog who decided to call the porch of the building his home. Before it was a restaurant, it was a house inhabited by schoolteacher Zoe St. Amand, who died in 1954. She is allegedly the cause of the present-day paranormal activity. Throughout the years, many claim to have witnessed her waving to them from the windows of Poogan's Porch. One patron of the restaurant even claimed to have seen an elderly woman staring back at her in the mirror in the first-floor restroom.

There are even police reports of eyewitnesses who reported somebody being inside the restaurant after closing. The reports are quite captivating. On numerous occasions, law enforcement officers entered the building to apprehend a reported trespasser. Yet after surveying the building, they never found anyone inside.

The Mills House Hotel is adjacent to the restaurant. Many guests of this hotel have reported seeing from their balcony a female in a black dress waving to them from the windows at Poogan's across the street. These are some of the reports that police investigated.

There are also various claims from the staff at the restaurant; most seem to involve objects being moved or going missing. Pots falling off the racks in the kitchens, doors opening and closing, objects being thrown mysteriously through the air, and random voices coming out of nowhere seem to be the norm inside Poogan's.

In November 2008, I decided to visit Poogan's Porch and conduct a night of research into the ghost of Zoe St. Amand. I arrived in Charleston at three in the afternoon and checked into the Mills House Hotel, since it was near the restaurant. Considering that many of the eyewitness accounts came from guests of the hotel, I found it fitting to put myself in their shoes and see things from that perspective. I requested a room with a balcony where I could view the restaurant.

Immediately after check-in, I stationed a few surveillance cameras on the balcony of my room, trained on Poogan's exterior. They began recording immediately and were left running until the next morning. My team would be joining me at the hotel later on.

As an investigator, I document everything. I decided to take a few photographs of the restaurant for documentation purposes from my balcony. The very first photograph I took was of the first-floor window, about two feet from the main entrance to the restaurant. To my surprise, I captured a very faint image of a female face looking up at me. I was astounded. I snapped a few more shots of the same area for verification, but no other photographs taken after that captured any similar images. At that point, I decided to venture over to the infamous location for a closer look.

It's policy at Poogan's Porch to leave the front door wide open during regular business hours, so I walked right in and went straight to the inside of that window. I found nothing tangible to explain the image of the face in my photograph. I am certain that at first the employees were wondering what exactly I was doing. Put yourself in their shoes: some guy bolts into their place of employment, completely ignores them, and starts examining a random window. Then, after freaking out the staff like I was some nut off the street, I asked to be seated for dinner. Although a little hesitant, they of course obliged.

The food at Poogan's Porch is exceptional and some of the best I have ever had the pleasure of consuming. It was there that I first tried alligator. The not-so-common dish was surprisingly tasteful. I recommend it.

I started asking my waiter, who had no clue who I was, random questions about the alleged sightings of Zoe St. Amand. He seemed happy to answer my questions and spoke of many experiences that guests have had, as well as the staff and even the owner of the restaurant.

Finally I introduced myself and explained why I was there. I had taken my camera into the restaurant with me, so I showed him the image I'd caught just moments prior. As his eyes widened in amazement, he politely asked if he could take the camera back to the kitchen to show the staff. Of course, I let him do so.

A few minutes later, the general manager approached my table with the camera. It was almost as if he were in a state of disbelief. He asked me if I'd taken that picture and I confirmed that I had. He told me that although he had never experienced anything paranormal in the restaurant, many have.

We chatted for a while about the logistics of the investigation, which I'd set up prior to coming to Charleston. He handed me a key to the building with brief instructions on how to lock up when I was done researching for the night. I finished a marvelous dinner and headed back over to the hotel to meet up with the rest of the team I'd assembled.

It did not take long for word to get out that I was in Charleston to conduct paranormal research at Poogan's Porch. I received a call from CBS affiliate WCSC-TV in Charleston, requesting permission to allow one of their news crews to accompany me during the investigation. That was not something I had ever allowed before; it always worried me that too many people involved in an investigation left too much room for contamination of evidence. The reporter promised me they would not get in the way and would only be there to document the research, so I agreed.

At approximately 10:30 that evening, my team and I left the hotel and headed into the restaurant to begin setup and preparation for the investigation. A few moments later, the WCSC-TV news crew arrived. Before we began the investigation, the reporter conducted short interviews with the team and me.

The news station wanted part of the segment to be shot live for their eleven o'clock news broadcast. Although I agreed, I was a little concerned that broadcasting live might place a "target" on the investigation. The last thing we needed was more onlookers.

After all of the press-related issues were out of the way, we started our investigation. As I noted earlier, the restaurant normally leaves its front door open for guests. This had me thinking that possibly birds or small animals could be the cause of pots falling from the wall and anomalous sounds in general.

Soon some activity started to present itself. We were all in the first-floor dining area at this time. My magnetic pickup started to sound off—a very strange and fluid percussive sound. It sounded like a woodpecker when it continuously taps a tree with its beak. Every one of us stopped and listened to this sound anomaly coming from my amplifier, hoping to hear a voice come through. Then, abruptly, it stopped. None of us had moved from where we were standing. A few seconds later, it started up again, only this time it was coming from the magnetic pickup another investigator was using. The sound had mysteriously jumped from my device to his. After a moment, it stopped once more. A few seconds later, two of our radios simultaneously started emitting the same tapping or clicking sound. Minutes later, the sound ceased and did not return until later that evening. We all considered this quite odd.

Next, I split up the team and we all sat in a quiet vigil in various spots throughout the building. I do this during every investigation. It gives us the opportunity to really *hear* the house and learn the little nuances of the place. After about an hour of inactivity, the team and I regrouped in the second-floor dining area. Not a single person had anything new to report at this point. We continued on with the research until close to two in the morning.

We were all gathered in the first-floor bar area when one of the investigators decided to check on the camera that we'd left upstairs recording in the second-floor dining area. He quickly returned, telling us that he found the camera powered off and completely drained of battery life. The battery that was powering that camera should have lasted at least four hours.

I decided to venture back upstairs to set up another camera myself, only this time I stationed it in the second-floor kitchen. This is known to be one of the hot spots in the restaurant for unexplainable activity. Reports have ranged from objects flying through the air to violent encounters with objects from the shelves hitting individuals. I stationed the camera so it covered the majority of the room. This would later prove to be a good decision.

As I was leaving the kitchen and walking back toward the stairway, I saw what appeared to be the shadow of a person shoot down the hall in front of me. Startled, I whispered down the stairs, instructing one of the other investigators to join me in the upstairs hall. Once he reached the top of the stairs, I explained to him what I had just seen. A second investigator joined us at the top of the stairs. The news crew remained on the first floor.

As we were standing there quietly, our radios started emitting that same strange clicking sound again, very briefly. We took one of the radios and placed it on top of the stair railing, and one of the investigators started asking questions. Almost on cue, the odd clicking responded as if answering his questions. We all agreed that it seemed as if something was attempting to communicate through the radios. Eventually the sound stopped, as if to end the conversation.

Upon returning to the first-floor dining area, our radios once again started emitting the clicking sound. So we decided to monitor this and log any useful data we might obtain. We placed all of the radios on one of the dining room tables. Beside the radios we placed EMF detectors, audio recorders, ion testers, and decibel readers. The sound grew louder as the session continued. Back and forth between every radio and amplifier we had, these sounds were conducting their own conversation.

I have to admit, I was a little frustrated. It really did feel like something was trying to be said; our equipment just could not get it out. I finally said, out loud, "I want a voice." Almost instantly, the clicking from the radios and amplifiers stopped, and a single word in a female voice came out of nowhere. This mysterious female voice said only one word: *Anna*.

I instantly asked the rest of the team if they had heard it, and they confirmed they had. It is important to point out that there was not a single female present that evening. Finally, we had received an undeniable attempt at communication. It remains unclear what the name Anna has to do with Zoe St. Amand or the activity at Poogan's Porch. But this incident sparked our excitement and breathed some much-needed energy into all of us.

It was now four in the morning and we all agreed it was time to pack up and conclude the investigation. I returned to the second-floor kitchen area to pick up the camera I'd left monitoring the room. When I arrived there, I noticed flour had been spread behind the camera. This caught my interest and I started reviewing the footage on the spot. Since the camera was facing the opposite direction, it did not capture who or what spread the flour around. It did, however, catch an amazing occurrence. On the back wall of the kitchen is a fairly obvious electrical box. To its right is a large exhaust fan sucking air out of the kitchen. A stainless-steel food preparation table sits in the center of the room. The walls are lined with shelves for supplies, and of course racks full of pots and pans.

The video captured a strange, concentrated light anomaly leaving the electrical box and flying across the room at a slow speed. The object was about the size of a quarter. Considering the amount of suction in the room from the exhaust fan, I immediately dismissed it being an insect of any kind. The object was actually flying *against* the current of that fan, and its flight pattern was unique. This pure white, circular light left the electrical box, flew across the stainless steel preparation table, did a loop, and then actually stopped in midair, hovering for a few seconds. If it had a personality, I would guess that it was recognizing the camera at the point where it stopped. From its hovering position, it proceeded to fly farther up into the air, until it was out of the camera's range.

Something else to note is that when the anomaly did the loop in the air, a distinct electrical sound could be heard. This same sound was also captured right before it stopped and hovered in midair. When it moved again, the sound continued. The electrical sound would either accelerate or decelerate depending on the object's movement. When it was slowing down to stop and hover, the sound decelerated. When it was taking off from its hovering state, the sound accelerated. I had never seen anything like it.

I returned to the first floor and finished packing up the gear. We locked up the restaurant and headed across the street to our hotel rooms. We were completely exhausted, yet excited about the productive research we'd conducted.

Poogan's Porch was well worth the trip. The food was fantastic and the night of research was even better. I hope to return sometime to investigate further. There is certainly something inside that restaurant worth pursuing.

THE HOTEL AIKEN

"Room 225" sounds like a horror movie title. The mysterious force inside this room, at the Hotel Aiken in Aiken, South Carolina, can drive a sane person mad. It has happened before and there is nothing to say it can't happen again. I have to admit that even I would rather not stay in that particular room for too long.

Originally called the Holley House, the huge, historic hotel was built in 1898 and has the oldest working elevator in the southeast. It is full of beautiful architecture, with a charming and enchanting feel to it. And, as one might suspect, the Hotel Aiken has its share of ghost stories and alleged paranormal encounters.

In February 2009, I started researching the hotel from my office, reading as much material as I could find on the building and its haunted history. I found numerous claims of paranormal activity. One common element to the claims was the reported haunting of room 225. Apparently, that room is so heavy in activity that guests staying in it typically call the front desk within an hour of checking in, asking to be relocated somewhere else in the building.

There are also a few reports of deaths on hotel property. It is believed that one of the original owners died in the building. It is also believed that a man committed suicide by leaping to his death from room 225. The claims about that one specific room really piqued my curiosity. For so many guests to request removal from that room, there had to be something explainable to justify it.

I called one of my investigators, who I'll refer to as Kevin, and suggested the hotel to him as our next assignment. He liked the idea, so we packed up the gear and drove three and a half hours to Aiken. I didn't call the hotel ahead of time, so I was taking a chance that they would be receptive to our investigation.

We arrived at the Hotel Aiken at approximately 3:30 in the afternoon. It was easy to find, since it's a historic landmark right in the middle of downtown Aiken. When I first walked into the lobby, I was impressed by its beautiful architecture and elegant atmosphere. I stood there looking around, admiring the rich and remarkable condition the hotel was in. The interior had a much different feel than the exterior of the building. I felt like I had stepped into another world.

The clerk at the counter was pleasant and courteous. I decided to slowly steer our conversation toward the real reason I was there. I started off by telling her we were journalists from Myrtle Beach, on site to report on the alleged paranormal activity the hotel is known for. She seemed excited to learn that paranormal journalists had driven nearly four hours to see the place. I explained that we wanted to conduct a full night of research in the hotel. She asked me if I needed to speak to the owner of the building, and I told her yes.

Not much time had passed when the owner approached me and shook my hand. I explained that we were there to conduct paranormal research within the building. Although he said he'd never had any personal experiences, he was aware of the claims and curious to learn whether there was any truth to them. He asked what I needed from him, and I said that I did not require much, just a tour of the place and two rooms to use as a base of operations.

The owner gave me permission to conduct research in the building. He told me that many had requested to investigate there in the past and, up until that point, he had never allowed anybody to do so. He knew my reputation, however, and gave us the go-ahead.

We were escorted to our rooms by the receptionist. She took us up on the famous crank elevator that is reported to be the oldest in operation in the southeast. Since I am an avid lover of history and antiquities, I found that to be quite a treat.

Around six in the evening, this same employee gave us a very thorough tour of the hotel. As a bonus, she even took us up into the attic so we could see how that old elevator actually worked. She was extremely informative about the history of the hotel and seemed intrigued by the possibility of the hauntings being validated.

She also took us into the room where the original owner allegedly died, which is now used only for storage; guests do not stay in it. She then escorted us into the basement, where one of the claims involved hearing music. When the elevator door opened, the three of us immediately heard music coming from the rear of the basement. When we approached the sound, we discovered it to be a radio. According to our guide, no one had been in the basement to turn it on.

I was so excited and engrossed in our history lesson and tour that I completely forgot to ask about the main reason we were there: room 225. At least I'd read a great deal about those claims before we arrived and figured I was as prepared as I needed to be.

We set up our equipment, and around 10:30 we started the investigation. Our plan of action was to do an initial sweep of every floor in the hotel to log baseline data from our equipment. I was surprised to find that electromagnetic fields were at a minimum for such an old building, and only high in the expected areas, such as around electrical boxes.

We started on the third floor with the plan of slowly working our way down. In one of the halls on that floor, I began to experience a slight case of vertigo. Both Kevin and I logged forty-two on the Gauss meter in that section. That was definitely well above the norm for a commercial hallway, and most likely the cause of my brief vertigo. As we continued down the hall, once again the EMF tester started registering a very high, abnormal reading. If we stood still, the high reading would go back down. But when we moved forward, it would start increasing again. It seemed that we were basically tracking a moving electromagnetic field down the hallway.

The meter led us right up to a door. At that moment, we both heard a very faint female moan. Just a few seconds later, we heard it again, only this time it was louder and more audible. Then, abruptly, the high reading on the EMF tester dissipated. The field was gone. The realization that we were standing outside the room the original owner had lived in and allegedly died in made this experience even more interesting.

Excited to have heard a phantom voice so early into the investigation, we left that area and continued back down the hallway. It wasn't long before the EMF tester started showing signs of activity again. The fields being discovered were always in the center of the hallway. The meter showed no signs of electrical interference when we swept the walls, ceiling, or floor. The field was strictly at chest-level in the hallway. Once again, we found ourselves being led down the hall and up to a door: room 320.

Once we got permission to go inside to investigate, we immediately noticed that the lamp on the desk was turned on. In fact, the whole room was lit up, which struck me as odd since no guests were staying there. Just as before, the EMF tester registered a high reading, only this time it was in the center of the bed. I also logged a temperature change; the center of the bed was eleven degrees cooler than the rest of the room.

As I was speaking with Kevin, who was logging this data, we both heard a female voice coming from just outside the door of the room. Both of our heads jerked toward the door. I ran over, swung it open, and jumped out into the hall. Nobody was there. The hall was empty.

We hung around a little longer in hopes of hearing the voice once more. As we stood there, the television set powered on, catching us both completely off-guard. The volume was turned all the way up and the channel display was nothing but loud white noise. We documented this strange occurrence with our video cameras as well as the EMF tester. The television was giving off electromagnetic fields far beyond normal for an electronic device of this nature. Typically, a TV such as this one would give off a 0.01 or a 0.02. During this time, it was registering 10 or higher.

We turned off the TV, and a few seconds later it turned itself back on again. Each time the television would power on, one of us would immediately turn it off. This occurred numerous times until finally the room became quiet once more. There was no rational explanation as to how it was powering on without human intervention. I found myself quite intrigued by this, since one of the claims mentioned televisions throughout the hotel powering on and off by themselves.

It was now midnight, and we ventured onto the second floor. I wanted to find the infamous room 225 and spend a large portion of the night in there. We walked all the way down to the end of the hall without incident and found an unmarked room with its door standing open. Upon going inside, I immediately felt uncomfortable and started experiencing slight nausea along with mild vertigo. Kevin shared the same symptoms I was experiencing. I knew that this discomfort wasn't coming from fear.

The room appeared to be an area for the housekeeping staff to store their supplies. But we could easily tell that at one point it had been a regular room for guests, with the typical layout and décor, and a full bathroom.

The room itself was the coldest area we had registered so far; the temperature was at fifty-two degrees. The hallways were at seventy-eight to eighty-two degrees, with some of the other rooms at a comfortable sixty-eight degrees. The hallways were not temperature-controlled, so any significant temperature change was easily noticed.

The door to the room stood wide open while we were in there. I happened to look out and across the hall, and saw that room 224 was adjacent to the room we were in. That meant we were standing in 225. Apparently it had been converted to storage since no guest would stay in it. The claims mentioned guests not lasting an hour in this room and now I could understand why.

As we stood there, our feelings of vertigo and nausea strengthened. Kevin even said he wasn't sure how much longer he could stand it. We got busy with our research regardless of feeling ill. As we were conducting EMF tests, we heard a faint sound of music. Initially we both dismissed it as coming from outside, but the music persisted and did not sound like it was coming from a car, or even a live band performing. We opened all of the windows to get a better listen. No music could be heard outside at all, just the ordinary sounds of the street below.

Although we opened all of the windows in the room and it was warm outside, the temperature inside held steady at fifty-two degrees.

Still struggling with the uneasy and uncomfortable feeling, we continued conducting EMF sweeps with our equipment. Suddenly our Tesla meters spiked to an unbelievable point: we registered a solid 130. That is extremely rare to see. Human beings can experience delusions, headaches, paranoia, and other symptoms from long-term exposure to a field as low as ten. This reading was thirteen times that amount—lucky us. The reading would swing from 120 to 140 while I was holding the meter completely still. Seconds later, the reading dropped and left us with nothing but a 0.01, which is the norm for any given room.

We had spent about thirty-five minutes in room 225 when the activity seemed to cease. We heard no more faint music; we got no more erratic readings on the equipment. It is hard to say whether I was just getting used to the uneasy feeling or it had gone away, but I was not as uncomfortable.

It was now 12:30 in the morning. We left room 225 and returned to roaming the hallways and investigating random empty rooms for more possible paranormal encounters. But the rest of the night was uneventful and we called it quits around 4:30.

In my assessment of the night's research, I concluded that paranormal activity appeared to have been present from 10:30 at night until 12:30 in the morning. During those two hours, we documented phantom female voices, drastic temperature changes, and extremely high electromagnetic fields.

The EMFs we logged that night remain some of the highest I have ever experienced. In most cases, fields stay in one spot, varying only slightly. At the Hotel Aiken, they actually moved, and on numerous occasions they moved down entire hallways, as if they were walking with us.

We found no explanation for the female voice we heard inside the room where the original owner had passed. The female voice coming from the third-floor hallway was also anomalous, and room 225 was the biggest puzzle of all. The significant cold temperature and the unexplained music would have been remarkable on their own. Adding to the mystery were the extraordinarily high EMF readings we experienced. Although I was unable to come to any solid conclusions about the cause or origin of the various strange occurrences, I felt as if we had validated the claims of paranormal activity at the Hotel Aiken.

9 WEBB MEMORIAL LIBRARY

Ghosts are something you read about in books, but what about those ghosts you find in a place full of books? There is something inside the Webb Memorial Library that checked in, but never checked out.

The Webb Memorial Library, located in Morehead City, North Carolina, has attracted a lot of attention within the paranormal community. Over the years, many people have reported hearing voices, finding objects moved, and even witnessing full-body apparitions. The director of the library has discovered books on the floor with pages ripped out and balled up. When opening the library in the morning, she has found books that were not there the night before, stacked neatly on tables. Paranormal investigators have reported phantom voices and objects moving. In the basement area, one group witnessed a bicycle flying across the room as if it had been thrown at them. Other researchers discovered that their stationary video cameras had been moved during investigations.

The building was constructed by Earle W. Webb, Sr. Construction began in 1929, but the building did not start out as a library. It was originally intended to be commercial space, with doctors' offices on the first floor and a training facility for a local garment factory on the second floor. Eventually the training facility relocated, leaving the second floor vacant.

Mr. Webb's wife was a member of the Morehead Woman's Club. When the second floor became available, she asked her husband if she could move the club's three hundred-book library into one of the available rooms. Mr. Webb agreed. Then, in 1936, their son Earle W. Webb, Jr. died of illness. To honor him, the Webb family dedicated the building as the Earle W. Webb, Jr. Memorial Library and Civic Center. The library celebrated seventy-five years of public service in 2009, with a collection of books that presently exceeds eleven thousand.

It was only a matter of time before I found myself becoming interested in this well-known site. My case manager for the North Carolina Division of the P.I.T. Crew started researching the library and the paranormal claims. In August 2009, she made the arrangements for the team to conduct a full investigation.

We were granted access to the facility for the entire evening, and met there about eight o'clock. A very nice gentleman greeted us at the door—a new employee who was quite curious about the paranormal claims. I'll refer to him as Oscar. He decided to observe our work.

First, we took a complete tour of the place to become familiar with the layout and to see firsthand the areas in which paranormal activity had been reported. The building consisted of two full floors, a basement, and an attic. The interior had an antique feel to it and each room was lined with books, ornaments, and framed portraits. A few rooms had beautiful chandeliers and long, conference-style tables. Others were filled with antique furniture and statues. Rooms on both floors were connected by long hallways.

Following the tour, we chose one of the first-floor computer labs as our base of operations and our rendezvous point for the evening. To my knowledge, no paranormal activity had been reported in that room. I decided to split the investigators into two separate groups. The North Carolina Division was one group; the other was composed of Oscar, myself, and two investigators, who I'll refer to as Dave and Connor. To start things off,

I stationed the North Carolina Division on the second floor, while my group started conducting work in the basement area.

There was not much to the basement at all: a couple small, musty, and damp rooms with electrical boxes and wiring scattered throughout. It gave access to a large crawl space, also full of endless electrical work. We noted the high electromagnetic fields coming off the electrical work with our devices. I also noted that somebody had written the word *boo* on one of the walls down there. We found that humorous, but detected nothing resembling paranormal activity.

I didn't feel the need to spend too much time down there, so we relocated to the first floor. The other group was still investigating the second floor. We moved to the far back section of the building where a circle of chairs was set up and decided to conduct a communication session.

We all sat down in chairs while monitoring the electromagnetic fields in the area. Dave documented the first strange occurrence. He pulled out his EMF tester and noticed the screen was fading in and out until it finally powered down entirely. I asked him if he'd placed a new battery in the device prior to the investigation and he confirmed that he had. A brand-new battery had somehow become completely drained, rendering his device useless.

I placed my EMF tester on the right arm of the chair I was sitting on. The reading was holding steady at 0.01.

On the left arm of the chair, I placed an analog audio recorder. We all started asking questions out loud in hopes of capturing a response on the recording.

As we all took turns asking questions, I asked that if someone was there, could they approach the device sitting on the right arm of my chair? A few moments later, the EMF tester went from 0.01 to 0.03. That wasn't a substantial increase, but considering the device was stationary, it could mean that a field had moved a little closer. I asked if something was there, could it move even closer? The device almost immediately went up another point, now registering 0.04, which was three points higher than the initial reading.

I decided to snap some random photos of the room. We were all still sitting in our chairs. I rarely use a flash during investigations, since doing so causes objects to cast shadows which can later be misconstrued. I was kind of surprised by one picture in particular. I had taken a shot of Connor, next to me, and it appeared that a solid black mass in the shape of a heavy-set person was standing right behind him.

I quickly showed the photo to the others, then took the EMF tester and started logging data behind the chair. That area was giving off a 0.18 on the Tesla scale, but there was nothing electrical nearby to have caused such a high reading.

We all looked at the photo in more detail. The baffling part was the fact that the black mass was not on the back wall of the room, where it should have been if it was in fact some sort of shadow. There was a good ten feet from the chair to the back wall. And if it were a shadow, it would have been much wider than it appeared in the photo. It actually was in the proper scale for a fairly large person standing upright. A closer look revealed what appeared to be curly hair on the head of the shadow, like that of a woman. Connor had extremely short hair cut military-style and was wearing a ball cap. The head of the shadow displayed no such traits.

I went behind the chair to check the EMF reading again. Surprisingly, the meter now read 0.01. This had me curious as could be. An interesting picture was taken with what appeared to be a woman standing behind an investigator, followed by a high electromagnetic field in the same spot. Now the field was gone.

While I was standing there discussing the photograph, I heard a faint jingle coming from out in the hallway. It sounded like either a chain rattling or a set of keys. Oscar, the library employee, did not hear the sound at first. Connor and Dave started to listen, and sure enough, all of us heard it then. This prompted us to vacate the room and enter the long hallway. We found nothing that could have caused the jingling sound.

From there, we decided to conduct some work in the children's section. This large room had hundreds of children's books, along with toys, games, and plenty of seating areas. There was also a checkerboard table, where we decided to sit and conduct another communication session.

Before beginning, Dave placed a surveillance camera in the corner of the room. I kept my video camera in hand so we would have two different perspectives. Dave and I sat across from one another at the checkerboard. Connor stood to my left, also filming with his video camera. Oscar sat on one of the couches at the other end of the room. He wanted to observe without contaminating any potential evidence.

Just as we were gearing up to start the session, we heard an electronic beeping sound. The EMF tester that previously had a drained battery had somehow managed to turn itself back on and appeared to be operating normally. We took note of this and moved on to conducting our communication session.

We placed three flashlights, a K-2 meter, a few audio recorders, and an EMF tester on the table, to the side of the checkerboard. At first we attempted to get the entity to play checkers with us. We were hoping to capture one of the checkers moving. Unfortunately, this was unsuccessful.

Continuing on, we started to direct attention to the three flashlights on the table. We asked random questions, asking the entity to turn the flashlights off and on in response. Again, nothing of significance occurred. I was beginning to think this room was inactive.

Finally, we asked if something was in fact in the room with us, could it move something on the table? Right afterward, Connor started talking. The two of us sitting at the table took our attention away from the session and started listening to him. It was at this moment that one of the flashlights slid across the table. We did not see this happen in real time since we were looking in the other direction. However, moments later, we looked down and noticed the flashlight was not where we had placed it. A quick review of the stationary surveillance camera showed that the flashlight had in fact been moved without human intervention. This was a great video capture.

After finishing up in the children's section, we could hear the other group returning to the first floor. We met with them in the computer lab to recount our experiences so far and to hear about theirs. Then my group decided to sweep the second floor while the other group maintained surveillance on the first.

We immediately began work in the first room to the left at the top of the stairs. I dubbed this the trunk room, due to the fact that it had a very old, authentic-looking treasure chest near the far wall. The walls of the room were lined with books, and various couches and chairs were scattered around the floor space. There was also a long wooden table with matching chairs near the end of the room, which we felt would be a good place to conduct a communication session. I placed a stationary surveillance camera on one of the bookshelves across from the table. Dave trained a surveillance camera on the same area from the corner of the room. We now had two different angles documenting the table area.

On the table we placed two flashlights, two audio recorders, an EMF tester, and a K-2 meter. Once we were ready to begin, the three of us took turns asking open-ended questions in hopes of gaining a response, either through a voice on the recorders or through the flashlights.

After about five minutes of asking questions to no response, Connor said he was starting to smell a woman's perfume. I quickly jumped out of my chair and walked around to where he was sitting. Dave did the same. All three of us acknowledged the faint scent of a perfume close to the table. To be certain, we called the other team, which consisted of all females, to ask if any of them were wearing perfume. They responded by saying not a single member of their group was wearing anything scented.

We wasted no time sitting back down and asking questions again. This time was more productive. I asked if the spirit present was a male. Nothing occurred. I asked if the spirit present was a female. Immediately the flashlight to my right powered on, then powered off shortly after. Believing that the spirit present with us was a female, I started addressing her as such.

Dave apparently desired a little more validation, so he asked once more if the spirit present with us was a woman. Just as before, the flashlight powered on. I later discovered on one of the audio recorders a disembodied female voice saying "Okay," directly after he asked the spirit to confirm its gender. This was an excellent audio capture, considering all females in the building were on the first floor. The voice on the recording sounded like it was right beside us.

I asked if the spirit had died in the building. Instantly the flashlight to my left powered on. Just to make sure this was not all coincidence, Connor asked if she was in fact confirming her death in the building. He asked her to turn on the other flashlight if this was true. The other flashlight lit up. All three of us were amazed.

We continued asking questions, and by means of turning the flashlights off and on, we learned that the female entity had died on the first floor of the building. She also told us there were five spirits in the library. During the entire session, the EMF tester was reading well over twenty on the Gauss scale. Once the session concluded, the tester dropped to 0.10.

Still on the second floor, we moved into the chandelier room. Can you guess why I called it that? The room was fairly large with display cases lining the walls full of ornaments, books, and random antiques. There was also a very long, conference-style table in the center of the room. We swept the area with our equipment first to log any abnormal readings.

We lined up three flashlights along the end of the table, and I placed a surveillance camera on one of the bookshelves to document the table area and the communication session we planned to do. Connor kept his camera in hand to document from his perspective. Oscar sat on a couch close to where we were conducting work. He was only a few feet from the end of the table.

Dave took the lead this time and stood at the end of the table. I stood near the doorway so I could keep an eye inside the chandelier room and an eye out in the hall behind us. As Dave asked questions, the entity wasted no time responding by means of the three flashlights. He would ask if the entity could turn on one of the lights. The light would turn on. He would then ask if the entity could turn the light back off. The light would turn off. This went on and on, and right on cue each time. The responses were so in tune to the questioning that Dave said he started to feel a little uneasy.

I decided to chime in by asking if this was the same female we had been speaking with in the trunk room. Once again, a flashlight flickered. I asked if she could turn that flashlight on again. Sure enough, the flashlight turned on again. We all stood there chuckling to ourselves, pleased with the responses. This is the kind of material that aids in building a solid case in favor of alleged paranormal occurrences.

After a few moments of silence, Dave told the spirit that if she could not do anything else, we were going to leave the room. As soon as he said that, the flashlight powered on once more. He turned and looked back at me. I could tell he was really feeling uneasy at this point and he admitted to feeling freaked out. This concerned me a little bit. For one, I do not want any of my investigators ever feeling uncomfortable. Secondly, his fear could potentially affect his judgment for the remainder of the investigation.

I needed to do something to bring him back to a comfortable level, and I knew that laughter would do the trick. I was still standing in the doorway when I noticed the dimmer switch for the chandelier on the wall. I waited for just the right moment. Dave was still facing the flashlights on the table. Connor was standing to my left, still filming, and Oscar remained on the couch. After a few moments of silence, with all attention on the table and flashlights, I quickly twisted the dimmer for the chandelier lights.

Obviously this created one hell of a spooky effect. The chandelier lights came on in a sudden burst of bright light. Dave, still standing in front of the table, jumped and shouted, "Look!" Almost instantly I burst out in uncontrollable laughter, taking claim to having turned on the chandelier lights. Dave, who was laughing now too, paced back and forth, a little worked up. He looked in my direction and jokingly called me an asshole.

This was a good stopping point and it was about time to meet up with the other group in the computer lab on the first floor. We packed up all of the gear and headed downstairs, where we all met up and shared our experiences. Of course, we had to share the chandelier incident, which everyone had a good chuckle over. Even Oscar shared in the laughter.

While all of the others were chatting away, I decided to step out of the lab and go explore a section of the library alone. Doing this always takes me back to the feeling of when I first started in this field. I'd always worked alone and now, even when working with a team, I still like to get away to fly solo for a spell. I left all of my equipment in the computer lab. All I had on me was a digital still-shot camera and a single flashlight. Later, I could have kicked myself for not grabbing a video camera.

I relocated to the far side of the library, away from the computer lab, and started taking pictures. I was standing in the long hallway on the first floor when I snapped an interesting photo. I realized I was standing right outside the room where earlier I'd captured that picture with what appeared to be a shadow standing behind one of my investigators.

The picture I had just taken shared similarities with the earlier one. In this one, there appeared to be a semi-transparent, heavy-set female walking down the hall. Whatever or whoever it was appeared to be wearing a dress. The photo from earlier showed curly hair on a heavy-set individual. This photo showed a heavy-set individual wearing a dress.

When I looked back down the hall with my own two eyes, nothing was there, yet the picture said otherwise. I started to walk back toward the computer lab to show it to the team. As I was walking past the stairs, I heard footsteps coming from the second floor. Without hesitation, I decided to investigate. I figured some of the team must have gone back up, but I wanted to be sure. I arrived at the top of the stairs and stood peering down the hallways, looking for flashlights or some indication a member of the team was upstairs. There were no lights in sight.

I proceeded to walk down one of the hallways with my flashlight on. This is where things took an uncomfortable turn. As I reached the end of the hall, my flashlight unexpectedly powered off, leaving me in complete darkness. I stood there for a moment before an intense wave of bitter cold air covered my body. It was an undeniable temperature change. I started to feel extremely uneasy. The occurrences we had documented earlier in the night did not have the same effect on me. I had a hunch that whatever was around me now was not the female we had successfully communicated with earlier. This entity felt negative.

Quickly I turned and headed back toward the stairs, using the little light that was coming up from the first floor to guide my way. I stopped at the top of the stairs to glance back down the hallway. At that moment, chills raced down my spine as from my left someone or something whispered, "Hey." It was not as simple as that, however. The word was drawn out slowly, as if being spoken while exhaling. It was creepy, and it sounded like it was right next to me.

I hurried down the stairs to grab a few members of the team and my video camera so we could further investigate what I had just experienced. I explained to all of them what had just happened and demonstrated that my flashlight was no longer operable.

Two investigators accompanied me back to the second floor. I took them to the exact spot where my flashlight had powered down and I felt the freezing cold air hit me. While we were standing there, my flashlight powered back on. The three of us looked at one another in amazement. They had seen me demonstrate moments earlier that the flashlight did not work. Now, all of a sudden it did, and I was not the one who turned it back on.

We remained in that area for a few minutes but discovered nothing abnormal. The cold spot never returned and our equipment was showing nothing out of the ordinary. Before we returned downstairs, I decided to station a surveillance camera on the stairwell, aimed in the direction where I'd heard that mysterious voice.

Very little happened after that, and certainly nothing any of us called paranormal. I told the team that I felt whatever was here had finished for the evening. I was pleased with what we had documented. We'd had multiple communication sessions that were productive, and we'd captured a few interesting photos. The other group had its share of experiences too, which were mostly similar to what my group had encountered—flashlight communication, cold spots, and even a rocking chair in the children's section moving as if someone was sitting in it.

Before officially calling it a night, I asked everyone to sweep the entire building one final time, just to be sure the activity had ceased. We all went our separate ways before meeting back at the stairwell. A few members were standing on the stairs; a few were standing at the top of them, while the remainder of the group was just inside a neighboring room.

Without warning, every radio we had started going haywire. It was like they were attempting to call each other, yet no investigator was pushing the buttons. Everyone had their hands where they could be seen. This was an odd occurrence, but only happened a few times. Metaphorically, I called it the buzzer officially ending the investigation.

The investigation of the Webb Library produced great results. Based on the seemingly endless flashlight communication and the disembodied voice on the recorder, I concluded that whatever is haunting the library is both aware and intelligent. We'd had a variety of other experiences, too: I'd heard a disembodied voice speak to me at the top of the stairs. We caught two unexplainable images on camera, had mysterious equipment failures, and saw a rocking chair and a flashlight moving without human intervention. When we reviewed the evidence, we noticed the stationary camera being moved in the children's section, as well as the female voice saying "Okay" in the trunk room. We'd also caught the phantom footsteps and the sound of jingling keys.

I doubt my research at the Webb Library is complete; I want to spend more time investigating the building. I can say with confidence that there are many paranormal occurrences taking place there. Further research might validate those occurrences or disprove them altogether, but I have a gut feeling that what is going on is real. One night of research produced way too much evidence for it to have all been coincidence.

My investigation of the Webb Memorial Library brought me full circle. Because of a story, I walked into a building lined with books in search of a ghost. Because of a ghost, I walked out with a story for my book.

10 THE NIGHTMARE SHOP

When you watch a horror film, you don't think that those ridiculous and frightening scenarios could ever be real, or could happen to you. A table saw turning on by itself, spinning those intimidating and jagged teeth that are capable of ripping you to shreds is not something you would expect to happen in your own house. But for a client of mine, it did.

Typically I am well prepared for any situation that fieldwork may present to me. I always conduct extensive research and preparation in the pre-investigation phase, since I've found these key elements play a pivotal role in the productivity and outcome of any given case.

Unfortunately, I took one case that granted no time to research or prepare for what I was about to walk into. I dubbed it "The Nightmare Shop." That name is fitting, considering that the investigation resulted in events straight out of a horror film.

I was familiar with the client beforehand, even though I had yet to fully research his case or conduct any work for him. For our purposes here, I'll refer to him as Bob. He and I had been discussing his case over the phone for a few weeks prior to my initial visit to the location. His claims were enthusiastic and outrageous, bordering on preposterous. He claimed that his carpentry workshop was haunted by a violent spirit that frequently made itself known by means of frantic and unrestrained confrontations.

The first time Bob became fully aware of the situation was when a table saw just a few feet away from him powered on without human intervention. He had also witnessed objects moving in the workshop, and even reported a hammer flying from the wall and landing a foot away from him. As always, I remained completely unbiased about the situation, at least until I could witness some activity myself.

Bob knew very little about the history of his property. He mentioned that the section of the house containing the workshop was constructed in the early 1900s; the rest of the building was added on and renovated numerous times throughout the years. He said that the activity only took place in the workshop and he had never experienced anything similar in any other part of the house.

On a night in September 2009, I was driving down the highway in my truck when I received a frantic phone call from Bob. Synchronicity being what it is, I found I was actually less than a mile from his house. He explained to me that, a few moments earlier, objects started moving in the workshop again and he no longer felt comfortable going into it. As soon as he'd walked into the room, an empty five-gallon bucket was mysteriously thrown at him.

I mentioned that I was close to the property at that moment and was willing to stop in for a preliminary look. With the activity being reported so promptly, there was a good chance I could witness exactly what he had been describing to me all this time.

I arrived at Bob's home within just a few minutes. I explained that I wasn't prepared to fully investigate his situation, but was willing to spend some time in the workshop to get a better understanding of the case. I asked if he could supply me with a few flashlights and he happily obliged. He took me to the entrance of the workshop and attempted to turn on the lights for me. The lights refused to operate. He was a bit surprised, considering that he was in the room just moments earlier and the lights were fully functional.

Of course, my suspicions were high. It all just seemed too perfect. I pressed on despite my gut feeling of a fabricated story and the possibility of foul play. I told Bob to remain in a comfortable part of the house while I spent a few hours inside the workshop.

I started by completely investigating the entire room to simply learn where everything was. More importantly, I wanted to locate any sharp objects or anything that could result in a dangerous situation if this was in fact a legitimate violent haunting. Bob had explained to me previously that the workshop did not have central air conditioning or heat. Two ceiling fans kept the room comfortable during the summer months and a portable floor heater provided heat during the winter months. This was good to know, just in case I noticed any significant temperature changes.

I immediately took note of random sounds coming from all different directions, like a light scratching against the walls. The first significant occurrence soon followed. I was standing fairly close to the door of the workshop when I started to hear a sound coming from the ceiling. When I looked up, I was surprised to discover the two ceiling fans were moving, each at its own speed. This was quite odd, considering the fans were off and no ventilation of any kind was coming into the room to move them. I stood still and filmed the fans until they eventually stopped turning.

I started to walk deeper into the room when, all of a sudden, a garden rake flew off the wall from behind me and nearly clipped me. Although it did not hit me, it did cause a little bit of a scare.

About an hour passed before something happened that convinced me of the importance and urgency of this case. I was walking around the room at that point; to my left was a thirty-gallon garbage can. My attention was completely drawn to the garbage can as I heard something move inside it. Of course, at the time, I thought there was something alive in there, probably a rodent. I stopped abruptly and waited for my camera to focus on the can. A few moments passed and I heard no other sounds. As I started to walk away and dismiss the incident, I was quickly turned around by another sound coming from that general area. Only this time, I saw the garbage can sliding ever so slightly across the floor.

Now I was really convinced something alive was in the garbage can. My first thoughts were of a raccoon or squirrel or some other kind of garbage-rummaging varmint. I slowly approached the can and aimed my camera down inside. To my surprise, it was completely empty. I could see nothing to have caused it to shift and move.

I did a complete 360-degree walk around the garbage can, just to rule out an animal being involved. Nothing was there. I started walking away again, and this time it slid even farther across the floor toward me. The sliding sound was much louder this time, and if I were to make an educated assessment of the situation, I would say that it was pushed or pulled in a violent manner. It was not eased across the floor—it was jerked quickly.

I ran over to the garbage can to examine it once again, but could not find anything to explain the movement. Then my attention shifted to the back wall, where I once again heard what could best be described as scratching. I started to walk slowly toward the sound for further examination. Again, I was leaning toward an animal being the culprit.

I was about halfway to the wall when the garbage can flew forcefully across the room, striking me from behind and causing me to nearly lose my balance. My heart was racing and my breathing escalated. There I stood, staring down at the garbage can that had incomprehensibly flown ten feet across the room, hit me from behind, and then fell on its side.

I was dumbfounded—scared, even. Typically I can keep my composure during situations like this, but the energy in the room was not positive. I felt completely unwelcome, since whatever was in there had no problem with letting me know that.

I stood there for a moment before walking around the trash can again in hopes of discovering a reason for the movement that did not involve spirit intervention. I found nothing—all elements pointed toward legitimate paranormal activity. I was excited and worried for the client, all at the same time. This was a unique event to have been witness to, and it certainly aided in validating Bob's claims.

I eventually set up the garbage can and slid it across the floor to its original location. Nothing else occurred. I stayed a few more hours before finally coming to the conclusion that the activity had ceased.

I met up with Bob outside of the workshop and reported what I had experienced. He was pleased to hear I was able to validate his claims. I told him I wanted to return soon with all of my equipment to research the workshop properly, and hopefully to find some answers to his questions about the activity. I showed him the footage of the garbage can moving and he did not flinch. He explained to me that the five-gallon bucket that came at him earlier had acted in the same fashion.

My advice to him was to steer clear of the workshop until we could better explain the activity, find a motive, and possibly discover a way to control the situation. I explained that whatever entity was residing inside the workshop was giving warnings, not full-blown attacks. There was a message being sent: whatever lies inside the workshop does not want people around. I told him that the activity could become much worse in the future if these messages were ignored.

I believe that something very dark is residing in the Nightmare Shop. When I think about that night, my heart races and my body wears a blanket of goosebumps. I remain concerned for my client and fear that he could be seriously injured. We have to face reality here: malevolent entities do exist. Although they are not as abundant as the mainstream media would like us to think, they are around us and they are not pleasant. I would rather face a lifetime of nightmares than face what lies within that shop again. But I will return. I will face it again. It is my job.

11 THE MUSIC HOUSE

Do ghosts enjoy music? It's hard to say for sure, but the presence of ghosts that are only active when music is being played seems to indicate that they do.

My team and I were contacted in October 2009 to perform a full investigation of the property I dubbed "The Music House." For years, the current owners had experienced active paranormal occurrences in the home. They believed that two spirits resided within. The first was that of a little girl in a long, wavy dress. The second was an older gentleman, distinguished and proper. The most unique claim about the activity was that these two spirits had an affinity for music. Almost always when music was present in the house, the spirits became active and did not hesitate to let the owners know.

One of the owners—I'll call her Carol—claimed that on one occasion, she actually felt a pair of hands press down on her shoulders while she was playing the piano. She turned around to see who it was, and nobody was there.

She believed that an antique piano brought into the home was one possible source of the activity. Many believe that entities or spirits can be "attached" to a certain object, such as a piece of furniture or jewelry; perhaps they owned that object in their previous life and refuse to part with it, even in the afterlife, no matter where the object may go.

Carol's house was originally used as a storage area for tobacco, after it had been cured in the barns and before it was wrapped, sorted, and delivered to the markets to be sold. The building was later used to store sweet potatoes. Workers would lay the sweet potatoes out on the floor, allowing the sun through skylights in the roof to cure them.

In 1981, the building was moved to its current location. Then it was converted in such a remarkable way that it was nearly impossible to recognize its original form. No one would ever know this private residence once stood in another town and was used for storing farm produce. Today the house is of average size, with the living area being the largest room. This was once the main section of the original building. Even the skylights and original woodwork remained.

Interviewing the clients revealed that the master bedroom, another bedroom on the first floor, and the room with the piano had the most activity, although they mentioned a few incidents outside of those rooms, as well. For example, in the kitchen, a glass flew off the counter and shattered on the floor right in front of Carol, and phantom voices were heard throughout the home.

While her daughter was away at college, Carol claimed that she would find her daughter's bedroom door open and the light on in the middle of the night, as if somebody were checking to see if she was home yet. This happened many times, and each and every time Carol would turn the light off and close the door. She believed that this was the spirit of the little girl checking on her daughter. There were also times when Carol would be awakened in the middle of the night by a voice telling her to check on her daughter.

Others often witnessed the activity, too. Carol's grandchildren showed signs of acknowledging the ghosts. She explained that her small granddaughter would stand with her back turned to Carol, with her arms up in the air, as if asking someone to pick her up. Her granddaughter was seeing somebody that wasn't there.

Finally, the clients showed me a very interesting picture, which truly aroused my curiosity in the case. This photograph of their granddaughter was taken near the piano room. A transparent white circle was surrounding her on the floor. Imagine a spotlight shining down from the ceiling, directly over the top of someone; that is what it looked like. Only there was no spotlight. Something unexplainable was captured in that image, and after thoroughly examining the room, I could find no logical cause for it.

After I'd heard all the paranormal claims, I scheduled a night to conduct research. Carol and her husband booked a hotel room for the evening, giving us total undisturbed access to the home. Since we were not talking about a lot of ground to cover, I only called on one other investigator to assist me.

My partner—who I'll call Tom—and I arrived at approximately eight o'clock. We used the kitchen as our base of operations, and started with a complete walkthrough of the entire house, making note of anything that might make noise or affect the temperature, such as air conditioning units and vents, timers, and floor creaks. Then we conducted a second survey to log electromagnetic field and temperature data before beginning the investigation work. The first hour was spent doing nothing but logging baseline readings throughout the house.

At first, I thought this was going to be an easy, open-and-shut case. In both the master bedroom and the daughter's bedroom, we noted high electromagnetic fields. We found the same in both the master bathroom and the daughter's bathroom. It appeared as though the clients possibly could have been suffering from the effects of overexposure to high EMFs, which could explain their perception of paranormal activity.

In the master bedroom, an alarm clock less than a foot away from the head of the bed was giving off an extremely high and constantly fluctuating electromagnetic field. Considering the average person is in bed for six to eight hours, that is a substantial amount of time to be exposed to such a field. Exposure can cause one to experience hallucinations and vertigo, among other things, and to hear voices.

Directly above the toilet in the master bathroom was yet another alarm clock, also giving off a high electromagnetic field. Now I had logged two areas where Carol was being exposed to these fields on a daily basis. In bed, high EMFs were surrounding her. In the restroom, they were directly above her head.

In the daughter's bedroom, we found that she, too, had an alarm clock directly by her head, and her bathroom had an even higher level of EMFs. This time the culprit was not an alarm clock. On the other side of the bathroom wall was the refrigerator. It was causing readings in the bathroom ranging from thirty to eighty on the Gauss meter—certainly more than enough to cause physical effects that would mimic paranormal activity.

I was starting to think our job was done here. In just a few hours, we were able to log enough data to justify the effects of high electromagnetic fields skewing the owners' perceptions. We were also able to debunk certain mysterious sounds as being caused by common mechanical devices. This was actually a typical residential investigation; normally, only a few investigations out of many produce anything paranormal.

The time was now 10:30, and we had only one thing left to do. We had been investigating the house for two and a half hours, and had never once brought the element of music into the investigation. Since the clients believed that music was what brought out the activity, we prepared to experiment at the antique piano, a spinet approximately waist high.

I stationed three cameras to document the mediocre performance that was about to take place—one camera to my left, one to my right, and another behind me. The piano was right up against a wall, so all sides were covered by the surveillance. I also put an EMF tester on the music stand of the piano so I could see any changes as I performed. Tom sat behind me, monitoring temperature-gauging devices.

I sat down at the piano and started playing various little melodies and scales, up and down the keys. I had only been playing for a couple of minutes when all three of the surveillance cameras monitoring the experiment powered down. This was truly amazing. One camera turning off could have easily been dismissed as a coincidence, but all three was beyond that. Each of them was running off fully charged batteries that should have lasted at least two hours. Instead, they only lasted about two minutes. I also noted a very large spike on the EMF tester in real time as the cameras went dead.

I quickly jumped up to examine the cameras. All three batteries were completely drained of power, and unfortunately, we had only these three video cameras with us. I ran back to the kitchen, where our equipment was, and grabbed a still-shot camera that filmed low-grade video as well.

I also grabbed the magnetic pickup and amplifier from my vest and turned it on. Both Tom and I were taken aback by the sound of a heartbeat immediately coming through the amplifier. The heartbeat sound was at its strongest around the piano, and was in perfect time, like a metronome. Soon the sound stopped and we sat in complete silence.

Immediately following this, we placed all of the video camera batteries on the chargers in the kitchen. As we were standing there discussing what we just had experienced, we both heard a low male voice coming from the daughter's bedroom. It was too low to make out any particular words but loud enough to give the sense of a man speaking.

Tom quickly and eagerly walked to the doorway of the bedroom. As he was standing there, I took out my still-shot camera and started snapping pictures of him in the doorway. To my surprise, something showed up in the picture with him. Above Tom's head was a strange mist-like or smoke-like mass that had no real defining shape. It was completely transparent. Since I had snapped multiple pictures standing in the same spot, we could easily see that this mysterious object was moving. Between the first and third photos, it had moved from above Tom's head to his left.

As we stood in the kitchen, amazed at the photographic capture, once again we both heard a low male voice. But this time it was not coming from the daughter's bedroom; it seemed to be coming from the living room. We went into the living room to investigate. We heard it again, and this time it was coming from the top of the stairs leading to the second-floor guest rooms. It seemed as if something was attempting to bait us, or lure us away from the daughter's bedroom. We went upstairs to investigate.

I could not help but think that once the music started, so did the activity. I kicked myself for not playing music early on in the investigation. But that is what makes me a paranormal researcher. I have to make every attempt to disprove the activity before I can make every attempt to prove it.

We continued on the second floor by investigating both guest bedrooms and the bathroom off the hallway. We found nothing of significance to explain the voice we kept hearing.

As we approached the top of the stairs to head back down, we heard a loud thud followed by a scraping sound. The loud thud actually made me jump a little. The sound was coming from downstairs somewhere. Once again we were being led by something we couldn't see.

We stopped in the piano room to talk a moment; I wanted to make sure the events so far had not clouded our judgment. During our conversation we both noted hearing a voice yet again. Like the first time, it was coming from the daughter's bedroom. I asked Tom to go check it out. I was going to grab the batteries from the chargers and fire up the video cameras again.

As I was loading the cameras, Tom yelled as if he were totally surprised and caught off-guard by something. He was standing in the doorway of the daughter's bedroom and I was about seven feet behind him, standing in the kitchen. The time was now 11:45.

I came up behind Tom with the fully charged video camera to see what he was excited about. My jaw dropped as my eyes focused on a chair in the center of the room that had not been there earlier. Previously it had sat at the computer desk. Very obvious dragging marks were visible in the thick carpet, extending from underneath the computer desk all the way up to where the chair now sat in the center of the room. Someone or something had moved the chair by dragging it across the floor.

Both Tom and I were dumbfounded. There had not been a single point during the investigation when he and I were separated. There was no opportunity for foul play or pranking to have been involved. Nobody could have entered the house without us knowing it. For a moment we were at a loss for words. Sometime in between me taking that photograph of Tom with the strange anomaly and going upstairs to investigate a voice, that chair was moved.

I noticed that the seat cushion of the chair was made of a fabric with musical notes as the pattern, another odd tie to the musical aspect of the paranormal claims. It was really creepy to stand there and see those drag marks on the carpet. That could have been the thud and scraping sound we heard while we were upstairs. Before we left the room, I trained a surveillance camera directly on the chair in hopes of capturing it moving again.

It was just after midnight when we heard another noise coming from the kitchen. We quickly ran to the kitchen and into the daughter's bedroom to see if the chair had moved, but it was still in the center of the room. Our EMF testers started registering high readings in the doorway to the bedroom. Earlier that night, when we had logged the baseline data of the house, there were no electromagnetic fields in that area.

The field moved along with us as we walked back into the center of the kitchen. I grabbed one of my flashlights and set it on the counter. I asked out loud if anybody was there with us, and no sooner did I say that than the flashlight powered on by itself. Then the electromagnetic fields diminished and the flashlight turned off almost simultaneously. The rest of the investigation produced no activity.

For about two hours from the point I played the piano, the activity was high and nearly nonstop. Tom and I played cat-and-mouse with the activity until that final experience with the flashlight. What had started out to be a typical residential investigation turned into so much more.

I waited about a month before scheduling another night of research at the Music House. This time, I decided to go alone. I started in this field alone and I actually love to conduct research work solo. On many occasions, I have found that being alone in an alleged haunted location can produce better results than having an entire team in there floating about. There is a certain intimate quality between a person and the spirits during one-on-one investigative work.

It was obvious at this point that the entity or entities present had the ability to move objects. Carol had told us of a glass in the kitchen flying from the counter and crashing to the floor. Tom and I had documented the chair moving in the daughter's bedroom. I made sure to have a surveillance camera running constantly on the chair.

Unlike the first investigation, when I almost completely ignored the musical angle to the activity, I decided to start the night by playing the piano. I stationed multiple video cameras around it to document anything that might occur during my performance. I also brought more cameras this time, in case the batteries lost power again.

I sat down at the piano and started to play. Just like before, every single camera in the room shut down at the same time. Last time I had played for about two minutes before this happened. This time, I was not even thirty seconds into a song before the cameras went down.

Once again I found myself gathering up the drained video camera batteries and heading back into the kitchen to place them on the chargers. I also grabbed one of the backup video cameras, but I was not going to play the piano anymore until those other three cameras were operable. I just did not want to risk missing any evidence. Twice now, music had invoked something that could completely drain those cameras of power.

Since I was in the kitchen, I quickly poked my head into the daughter's bedroom to check on the camera watching that notorious chair. Everything seemed all right and I proceeded into the living room. I sat on the couch for about ten minutes before hearing a low murmuring sound coming from upstairs. Of course, I went to the second floor to investigate.

When I walked into the first guest room on the left, I could have sworn I briefly heard a little girl's voice. It stopped me dead in my tracks. I noted a spike on the EMF tester at the same time. I waited in that room for a few minutes before hearing yet another voice coming from downstairs.

I slowly went down the stairs in hopes of catching something off-guard. I constantly remind myself that spirits or entities were once human, so in theory they should think like humans. If something were attempting to hide from me, I had to be more covert. This time I did not have another investigator with me, making conversation. This time I could be more inconspicuous, and hopefully catch what was causing this activity.

I was almost to the bottom of the stairs when I heard a very faint, high-pitched sound coming from the piano room. It sounded just like one of the high notes from the upper section of the keys. I leaned over the banister so I could see the piano in my camera's viewfinder. I stood there briefly and did not hear the sound again.

I came down the last couple of stairs and decided to quickly check on the camera in the daughter's bedroom again. Just like last time, nothing had changed. The camera was still recording and the chair had not moved an inch.

I left that area and proceeded back into the piano room to investigate what could have possibly made that sound. With the weather outside getting warmer, I knew it was very common for objects made of wood to shift and expand. Since this piano was made almost entirely of wood, I could not rule out humidity shifting something and causing one of the strings to be stretched, resulting in a random sound.

I stood there, keeping the entire piano in the frame of my camera. As I was documenting the situation, another note was played right in front of me, but there was nobody there to play it. I was literally standing directly in front of the piano at the time. There was no mistaking that the note came from that piano.

A few seconds later, another note was played. This time, however, my camera actually caught something quite significant. On the video, I could see a slightly transparent silhouette come up from the right-hand side of the piano and touch a key. At the same time, a note was played. I could not believe what I had just captured, and it was directly in front of me. You have no idea how tickled I was to have this paranormal occurrence captured on film.

I waited a little while longer, but not another note was played. The time was now approximately eleven o'clock and the investigation was showing some really great productivity. I decided to set up a communication session in the living room. It seemed like whatever was there might be opening up to me during this second investigation. I felt like they knew who I was and what I was there to do.

I sat down on the couch, placed a flashlight on the coffee table directly in front of me, and trained my camera on it. The flashlight was in the off position. At the beginning of every communication session I conduct, I always announce myself the same way: "My name is Stephen Lancaster and I am a paranormal researcher." It's straight to the point.

I started asking random questions and kept drawing attention to the flashlight on the coffee table. I wanted to film interactivity with that flashlight. I instructed whoever was there to use it to communicate with me. I told him or her that all they had to do was make it come on to answer my questions. The entity wasted no time responding to me. I asked if it was in the room with me, and the flashlight quickly powered on and then immediately powered off. I felt I was making progress.

Call it a hunch, but I believed that the spirit I was communicating with at that point was the little girl the clients had spoken of—the same little girl I believe I heard speaking upstairs earlier that night. I continued to ask questions and, each and every time I did, the flashlight would flicker on and off, right on cue. Then I asked if she liked it when I played music. The flashlight came on so bright that it shot a line across my camera screen.

During normal operation, its light was never that bright, but this flare made me see spots.

I came off the couch and crouched down a few inches away from the flashlight. I wanted to get a better view with the camera. I kept asking questions, but this time the flashlight was unresponsive. Finally, I asked if I were making her uncomfortable by being so close, and the flashlight flickered on and off as if to confirm my assumption. I quickly moved away and sat back down on the couch.

The reason I believe I was communicating with the little girl spirit was because of the timid behavior that occurred once I moved closer to the flashlight. To me, that just seems like something a little girl might have done. I sat there on the couch collecting myself. I was extremely pleased with that communication session. I turned the camera on myself and quickly gave a verbal recap of the events that had just occurred.

Once again, I heard a voice coming from the daughter's bedroom. I quietly pulled myself off the couch and crept across the living room. I was only a few feet from the bedroom door when I noticed a significant change in the temperature. It was much colder outside that door now than it had been before. With no air conditioning vents to explain the change in temperature, I knew I was close to something.

As soon as I entered the room, the flashlight from on top of the surveillance camera flew off and struck me in the chest. I was completely caught off-guard and the video showed that. Shocked, I very cautiously peered around the room and even into the bathroom. There was nothing to be seen.

Was the flashlight flying at me a warning? I believe so. I think at that point I was dealing with the gentleman spirit, and he was telling me to vacate the house. I got the impression he thought I had seen enough already and did not need to see more. I felt like my interactions with the little girl spirit and the older gentleman spirit were quite different. Where the girl was playful, the man was more standoffish. He was telling me it was time to go and I agreed wholeheartedly. I slowly backed out of the bedroom and began packing up my gear.

A second night at the Music House had provided substantial evidence to support the claims of the clients. Capturing the anomaly striking the keys on the piano still is a highlight for me. That was simply incredible. The communication session with the flashlight led me to believe that the entity there was feeling comfortable with me, but after I was attacked by the flashlight in the daughter's bedroom, I knew I needed to show respect and leave for the night. I was building a relationship with these spirits and did not want to do anything to mess that up. I knew it would be only a matter of time before I found myself back there to investigate once again.

———————

They say that the third time is a charm, and I believe there is some truth to that statement. Months later, Carol asked me to return. She said the activity had been at high levels and the voices at night were becoming more frequent.

I brought another investigator with me who had not been involved with the case before; I'll refer to him as Gary. The clients let us into the house as they were leaving for another night in a hotel room. We arrived at eight o'clock in the evening, set up our equipment, and took initial readings, as usual.

We kicked things off by splitting up at approximately nine o'clock. Gary covered the second floor bedrooms and bathroom, while I focused on the first-floor master bedroom and the daughter's bedroom. We both had video cameras running.

After about forty-five minutes of being separated, Gary called me on the radio to ask if I had been talking or recording a monologue at the bottom of the stairs. I said that I had not and was in fact in the master bedroom, which was the farthest away from that area. He said that he could hear voices coming from the bottom of the stairs and described it as being like the sound a television makes through a wall from another room. He said the voice was muffled, yet loud enough for him to determine it was a man's voice he was hearing. Again, even though

I was quite a distance from the stairs, I confirmed that I had not said one word aloud since we separated.

A little while later, I met back up with Gary and we traded floors. He mentioned that he had experienced a few unexplainable occurrences while he was on the second floor. He did not give me specifics, though, since he did not want to influence my perceptions. He advised me to simply go back and forth between the two guest bedrooms.

I took his advice and moved back and forth between the two rooms about every fifteen minutes. I was finding nothing out of the ordinary. Every piece of equipment I was using returned normal results. Meanwhile, Gary was documenting a strange scratching sound coming from the bathroom off the master bedroom. He described it as like somebody taking their fingernails and dragging them across the wall.

At eleven, we met up outside of the house to take a quick break, collect our thoughts, and discuss the investigation so far. Our conversation ranged from the high electromagnetic fields that the household alarm clocks gave off to the client's dog. Seeing the dog box outside prompted Gary to ask if the dog was here, which could have explained the scratching noise he had documented moments earlier. I assured him the dog was not present and we went back inside to continue our work.

Gary proceeded back upstairs to see if he could experience again whatever he had experienced before. I kept my focus on the first floor. The activity had yet to really come out into the open. I continued researching in the master bedroom, since the most recent claims of hearing voices came from that room. Upon entering it, I noticed almost immediately the very faint sound of an alarm clock repeatedly going off. It went on and on without stopping. I searched the entire bedroom and even the master bathroom for the alarm clock that I was convinced was the culprit. The strange thing about it was that no matter where I went, between the master bedroom and bathroom, the sound stayed at the same volume. There was no sense of distance or closeness to the alarm, since it never fluctuated in volume.

After about ten minutes of this, I called Gary on the radio to see if he could hear the phantom alarm going off. He said no, then mentioned that he had just heard a low growl coming from somewhere upstairs and described it as sounding like a dog.

I instantly remembered our earlier conversation about alarm clocks and the client's dog. I was beginning to think that someone or something had overheard us and was now making these things mysteriously come to life. Either that, or it was one weird coincidence. I decided to stop my camera and play back the recording from the past few minutes. Sure enough, the alarm sound was present on my camera's audio and I could rest assured that I was not imagining it.

With the alarm sound still present, I went back into the master bathroom, still looking for the source. Again, the alarm sounded exactly the same here as it did out in the bedroom. The master bathroom is quite long with double sinks, a shower, and a good-sized tub area. There is also a full walk-in closet at the very back, about ten feet from the entrance to the bathroom.

I was almost to the walk-in closet when the door to the bathroom started to close. I could hear it closing behind me, so I turned around with the camera as fast as I could. I was able to capture the last few seconds of the door closing. The unsettling part was the fact that after the door closed, I could clearly hear the sound of somebody latching it from the other side. I ran to the door and grabbed the handle, throwing the door wide open. No one was there.

I immediately called Gary on the radio and asked him to join me in the master bedroom. I met him halfway, in the living room. Curious, he quickly asked me what had happened. I told him more about the alarm clock sound and then described the situation with the bathroom door closing behind me. I showed him the footage of it on my camera. He was just as amazed and excited as I was. Then he started to tell me more about hearing the low growl upstairs. Honestly, I thought maybe he simply heard his stomach growl from being hungry. I would later find out that this was not the case.

We decided to stay together and proceeded to the second floor. We stationed ourselves in the first guest bedroom to the right of the stairs. While we were conducting a communication session, Gary started to tell me what he had been experiencing in there. He said that anytime he was in that room, his body would become overcome with exhaustion. Many times he had caught himself nodding off, which was really out of character for him. He told me that the feeling of exhaustion did not happen in any other room, only the one we were sitting in. While we were sitting there, I noticed how frequently he was yawning and fighting to hold his eyes open. It was interesting to witness, considering I felt completely normal and unaffected by whatever was draining him of energy.

We decided to walk over to the other guest bedroom to see if anything was happening there. Gary was in front of me monitoring the EMF detector. As soon as he stepped foot inside the room, the detector spiked quickly up to a four on the Gauss scale. He stopped suddenly to show me, and I told him that I had heard a little girl's voice in there during the previous investigation.

The electromagnetic field dropped back down to zero in the center of the room. Gary started checking other areas of the room with the detector. As he approached the dresser, the reading spiked again to a four on the Gauss scale.

I was standing to his right, filming to document the sudden and sporadic changes in the EMFs of the room. As my camera was trained on him, I caught something moving slightly out of the corner of my eye. I turned my head to look and was shocked at the sight of a little girl walking past the foot of the bed. It startled me so much I actually gasped. (I am not really a gasping type of guy and up until that moment I can say with confidence that I had never gasped before in my life.)

Of course my reaction immediately caught Gary's attention, and he was quick to ask what was going on. I told him what I had just briefly seen. As I had turned my head, the little girl had started walking down the side of the bed and then vanished.

We quickly moved to that area of the room to check for any abnormal electromagnetic fields and temperature changes. No temperature changes were logged, but we did note a few abnormal EMFs around the side of the bed. Nothing electrical was nearby to justify the readings and as quickly as the fields came, they were gone.

Gary went back toward the dresser he was previously investigating. In the center of the room, a four on the Gauss scale registered again on the EMF tester. We had now noted this strange field in multiple spots in the room. I had just walked up behind Gary when we both heard a light, brief, sliding sound coming from the dresser. We both stood there staring at it, waiting for something to happen—and it did.

The far right, top dresser drawer was slowly opening as if somebody was pulling it. I could not believe what I was seeing, and filming, just a few feet in front of us. I crept a little closer to make sure the camera had the best view possible. The drawer continued to open very slowly until it stopped about three-quarters of the way out. I stood there in total amazement. After a few minutes, it was clear the drawer was not going to move again. I pushed it shut and started stomping around the room and even shaking the dresser to prove a vibration was not the reason that drawer had opened. I was unsuccessful at finding a logical solution. Considering that we had logged abnormal electromagnetic fields and I had seen what I believed to be a little girl, it was not too hard to believe that the drawer opened by itself. This was one for the books.

We shifted our focus to the daughter's bedroom on the first floor. We were talking when I heard a low growl coming from above me, as if a dog were hanging out on the ceiling. I looked at Gary and he acknowledged that was the same sound he had heard earlier upstairs. The daughter's bedroom was directly below the guest room he had heard the growl in.

It was now one o'clock in the morning and we agreed it was time to conduct a lengthy and sincere communication session. We went back to the living room and we both sat on the couch. I placed a digital still-shot camera on the coffee table in full view of both of our recording video cameras. The audio recorders were running and we were filming the session from two different angles.

I asked the spirit if he or she was in the room with us. On cue, the digital camera turned itself on, right in front of us. I asked if he or she was the one who shut the bathroom door on me earlier in the night, and the camera turned off as if to acknowledge my question. This went on and on over the next few minutes. Each time one of us would ask a question, the camera would either turn on or off in response.

Next we asked if he or she could come closer to the coffee table. No sooner was the question asked than Gary reported that his video camera had turned off and was drained of battery life. We were now filming with only my camera. We continued with the communication session without getting any further responses. It seemed like the spirit had left us following the battery drain on Gary's camera.

We sat there for a few minutes in silence. The digital still-shot camera was still powered up on the coffee table. I finally stated that if he or she would turn off the camera one more time, we would pack up and leave. Right on cue, just like the times before, the camera turned off by itself.

I grabbed it and tried to power it back on, but was unsuccessful. The battery life had been drained.

Keeping our word, we packed up all of the gear and loaded it into the vehicle. Just as we finished, I remembered that I had left the still-shot camera in the living room on the coffee table. We both went back into the house to get it. Just out of curiosity, I decided to hit the power button, and to my surprise, the camera powered on without hesitation, indicating the battery was fully charged.

During the drive home, we discussed how productive the third night of research at the Music House had been, even though we never got around to playing the piano. Gary was amazed at how that guest room could drain all of his bodily energy every time he went in it, and to this day I cannot believe I saw a little girl standing at the foot of that bed, but I did. Months prior, when I had originally accepted the case, I was expecting a simple sweep-and-debunk investigation like so many residential investigations are. This case turned out to be so much more.

Today, the clients are great friends of mine, and I cannot stress enough how much I appreciate them allowing me to continue conducting research in their home. I know my findings have eased their minds. The spirits within that house show intelligence, and music seems to be the best tool to reach them with. It is ironic, when I consider the thousands of dollars of equipment I use to research the paranormal, that something free like music ended up being the most useful tool in this case.

The Music House remains one of my favorite places to investigate. Now, if I could just get that little girl on film ...

 12 BRENTWOOD WINE BISTRO

Typically, when you look in the mirror, you see a very familiar reflection. This is true even for ghost hunters—most of the time. However, on one memorable occasion I looked into a mirror and saw another person's face looking back at me. I was face-to-face with a ghost.

In Little River, South Carolina, there is a magnificent, charming, beautiful, historic restaurant called the Brentwood Wine Bistro. Low Country-French cuisine is its specialty. The food is to die for (no pun intended) and the building has a natural magnetism that will draw you to it. The house the restaurant operates out of is over one hundred years old and has an unusual history.

This location is becoming famous for its haunted atmosphere. In the fall of 2011, the A&E Biography show *My Ghost Story* interviewed the owner of the building and me for a special segment on the ghosts of Brentwood Wine Bistro.

I have to tell you that this location has been the pinnacle of my studies as a paranormal researcher. I have been researching in this building off and on for over a year and consider it the most active location for paranormal activity that I have ever been in. Keep in mind that I have conducted work in some of the most widely known and commercially advertised haunted locations.

The house was built in 1910, and the original owner resided in it until she passed away on August 15, 1974. Her husband had died at an early age in the 1940s. After his death, she converted the house into a bed and breakfast. The cost was one dollar a night and an additional fifty cents to have breakfast included. In the early 1970s, she was approached by a local businessman who wanted to buy her house, demolish it, and use the land for a business.

The widow was very passionate about not wanting the house destroyed. Many believe it was because her late husband's spirit was still present in the house and she knew that. Since she was so adamant, the businessman agreed to move the house across the street to free up the land. Every piece of it was relocated, which is a rarity. Normally, when a house is picked up and moved from one location to another, the foundation and stonework, such as chimneys, are rebuilt. In the case of the Brentwood, the entire structure was moved. Today, the Brentwood sits on Luck Avenue. You may not see the significance of that now, but you will.

The widow spent the remainder of her years in the house. Then, in the late 1970s, it was converted into a country-style restaurant called Grandma Mary's. In the 1980s, it was purchased and restored to its natural beauty before being turned into the Brentwood Restaurant by two brothers from Brentwood, New Jersey (hence the name). One coincidence regarding the history of this place is the fact that the Brentwood opened its doors on August 15, 1991, seventeen years to the day after the widowed owner's death.

It is believed that there are two spirits haunting the Brentwood: the original owners of the house. Employees and patrons of the restaurant have experienced doors opening and closing, hearing female voices when no women were in the building, and even seeing physical manifestations they described as solid black, three-dimensional, shadow-like entities.

The current owners of the restaurant are well aware of the paranormal activity. Shortly after they took over operations, they started experiencing unusual occurrences.

But it wasn't until one of them—I'll call her Kathy—met with a previous owner that she became curious about the haunted atmosphere. Kathy asked the previous owner if she had ever experienced anything abnormal within the house. The previous owner told her that there were two ghosts that appear to be walking shadows, and she had become so used to the activity that she referred to the ghosts as part of the family.

This is the part of the story that really grabbed my attention. The current owners had no prior knowledge of the haunted history of the place; they discovered the activity on their own. In many cases, being influenced by a ghost story can make you think you are seeing something that is not really there, or make you see what you want to see. With the current owners, however, there was no opportunity for them to have been influenced.

It is evident when walking through the interior of the restaurant that the current and previous owners believed something unearthly to be present. In every room, paintings and pictures of angels grace the walls. Angels are also carved in the wood on many doors throughout the building. Some say those angels were placed there as a form of spiritual protection, while others say they are unrelated to the house's history.

When I first made contact with the current owners, Kathy was seeking validation for the paranormal occurrences. She told me of the shadow entities often seen by her and the staff, the disembodied voices they heard, and the odd photographs taken by patrons, in which unexplainable images appeared that were not there at the time the shot was taken. Kathy even has a collection of many photographs containing possible paranormal phenomena.

After hearing all of the claims, I was biting at the bit to spend a full night in the Brentwood. A place allegedly that active is any paranormal researcher's dream to investigate. I quickly set a date for the initial night of research work, and in January 2010, I first stepped foot inside the bistro.

I arrived with an investigative team of three, including myself, about an hour before the restaurant was to close for the night. This gave me time to interview the staff and hear their claims firsthand. They were all very passionate in telling of their encounters with the ghosts.

The owners gave us a guided tour of the building, showing us the areas in which they and the staff had witnessed paranormal activity. One of the owners was very receptive to the activity, while the other just tried to ignore it. Neither of them appeared to fear anything, however.

The bistro cleared out for the night until only the owners and a few staff scheduled to close up remained. One employee in particular almost came to tears when she had to go back upstairs to power down the building for the night. She actually asked us to escort her to the second floor so she could switch the power off. She seemed truly frightened to go anywhere alone in the building, so of course we followed her upstairs so she could do her job.

Before leaving us to it, the owners gave me instructions on how to lock the place up the next morning when we were finished. The Brentwood does not open on Sundays, so we had the luxury of taking all the time we needed. Next we went out to our vehicles to bring in all the equipment. Since the first dining area to the right had no activity reported in it, I decided to use it as our base of operations. At approximately midnight, the owners left for the evening and the three of us could begin work. I'll refer to my investigators as Chuck and Brad.

I decided to train a surveillance camera on the areas where the shadow entity was reported. The most common sighting took place in between the second-floor bar and the bathroom. Not only had the shadow entity been seen in this area frequently, but many patrons of the bistro had also reported becoming trapped inside the bathroom. They described feeling like somebody was pushing on the door from the outside, preventing them from opening it. I stationed a video camera on a tripod and aimed it toward the bathroom door. Since it was going to be running all night, I plugged it into a nearby outlet so as not to waste battery life.

The building was pitch black inside. The first room we investigated was the second dining area to the right. During the tour, the owners had claimed that the lights on the chandelier in this room would flicker off and on, and the chandelier would even swing when they tried to remove a framed picture from the first-floor bathroom wall. The picture appears to be a husband and wife posing for a portrait. It had been left in the building by the previous owners and probably pre-dates their ownership.

Kathy told us that the picture had an undesirable quality that disturbed people, and she wanted to remove it from the bathroom wall. However, each time they attempted to move it, the second dining room to the right showed increased activity. She claimed that when they put the picture back on the wall, the activity in that room would cease. She also informed us that the closet door in that room would open and close on its own.

I started with the closet door, experimenting to see how easily it would open and shut. It was very stiff and took a great deal of force to move. Even when I swung the door wide open, it would catch about halfway and I would physically have to push it all the way closed. I latched the door closed and we all made note of that.

From there, we moved into the first-floor bar and then into the third dining area. The place seemed quiet. I took the team into the kitchen where, like the rooms before, we made note of electrical work giving off electromagnetic fields. It was much warmer in the kitchen area, mostly due to the ovens that were still cooling down. We were all sweating at this point, so any type of significant temperature change would certainly have been noticed.

After logging as much data as we could in the kitchen, we decided to venture to the second floor, where we did a full sweep of the bar and the dining rooms. While Brad and Chuck looked for a logical reason why patrons were getting trapped in the second-floor restroom, I decided to return to the first floor.

The first-floor restrooms, where the mysterious picture mentioned earlier was located, are at the bottom of the stairs and to the right. When I arrived at the bottom of the stairs, the men's room door suddenly closed. I trained my video camera on the door and watched as it slowly opened back up and then closed again.

I had examined that door previously, during my initial sweep of the building. It would not remain open without someone holding it open. The hinges were very loose. I could push the door open, but it would immediately close. So standing there and watching it open and close, seemingly on its own, was interesting. I walked in front of the door and noticed immediately how significantly colder it was in that spot. A burst of cold air came pouring out of the bathroom when I opened the door to investigate.

Meanwhile, back on the second floor, Brad and Chuck were still attempting to figure out what could be trapping patrons inside the bathroom. As Brad was exiting the bathroom, he heard a voice come out of nowhere. This was in the same spot where Kathy told us they would often hear a female sighing. He asked Chuck if he had just heard somebody say something. Chuck said he thought the voice was Brad and was surprised to find out it was not. They quickly came down the stairs to find me.

I was walking out of the men's restroom when they arrived at the bottom of the stairs. Before they could tell me about the voice they'd heard, I told Brad to stand in front of that bathroom door. He immediately noticed the coldness surrounding it. Chuck pushed the door open and confirmed the bitter cold pouring from inside. Earlier that night, the restroom had been logged at 0.01 on the EMF tester. Now, when he walked inside, he logged a seven on the right-hand side of the room. Moments later the reading dropped back down to baseline, then he caught the seven again on the left-hand side of the room. It seemed as if something had moved across the restroom and back toward the door. Then suddenly the EMF tester dropped back to 0.01 with no further fluctuations.

The time was closing in on one in the morning. I instructed Brad to station himself at the bottom of the stairs, where he could see the second-floor landing and the first-floor restrooms. Chuck and I decided to go back to the kitchen. As we walked into the center of the room, both of us noted how cold it was in there. An hour earlier we had been sweating in the kitchen, and now we were freezing. All of a sudden, a very loud crashing sound came from a few feet in front of us. It sounded as if somebody had taken a hundred pots and pans and dropped them on the kitchen's tile floor. It startled me so much that I jumped back about three feet and shook the camera.

On the radio, I called Brad and instructed him to join us in the kitchen. He arrived swiftly and I explained what had just happened. He, too, had heard the loud crashing sound, even though he was all the way out in the front of the bistro. He said he thought one of us had knocked something over by accident. I assured him that was not the case and showed him the video footage I'd just taken. It showed absolutely nothing in front of us, yet the sound of crashing pots and pans came out of nowhere.

This prompted Chuck to start asking questions out loud, directed toward the unseen force. Brad went outside and around to the back wall of the kitchen. He pounded on the wall from the outside in hopes of being able to rec-reate the noise, but was unsuccessful. The crashing sound remained a mystery.

Brad came back into the kitchen while Chuck was still attempting to communicate with what could have been the ghost. Both Brad and I took note of a light, high-pitched sound coming from outside the door into the adjacent bar. We crept over and placed our ears on the door to hear a little better. It sounded like wine glasses were being clinked against one another. Brad slowly opened the door so we could see into the first-floor bar area. Spanning the entire length of the bar itself was a wine glass rack. The wine glasses in it were swinging ever so slightly and touching one another, causing the sound we were hearing.

I called Chuck to come and help us investigate the mysterious moving wine glasses. I noted that they were giving off an EMF reading of ten on the Tesla scale. They gradually stopped moving and I lost the field on my detector.

Within our first hour of research, we had experienced a phantom voice on the second floor, the men's restroom door opening and closing with a significant temperature change around it, an unexplained crashing sound in the kitchen, and now wine glasses swinging for no apparent reason in the first-floor bar area. The night had been very interesting so far.

As we were leaving the bar, Chuck pointed out that the closet door in the second dining area was wide open. We all knew I had closed that door and latched it. This time I took a chair from underneath one of the dining tables and shoved it up against the door. There was no way it could come open now without a great deal of force.

We left that dining area and headed back to the second floor. When I arrived at the top of the stairs, I immediately noticed that the camera I had left monitoring the restroom was powered off. The switch on the camera was still in the on position, yet the camera had no power, even though it was plugged into an electrical outlet. There was no battery to go dead in this situation. I dismissed this as due to a faulty outlet and flipped the switch off then back on again. The camera powered right back up as if nothing had ever happened.

I decided to review the tape to see at what point the camera had lost power. It was difficult to see, but it appeared as if some sort of shadowy mass came out of the bathroom toward the camera. About the time it passed the camera, recording stopped and all power was lost. I couldn't wait to get home to review that on a bigger screen.

At this point, Brad needed to replace the battery in his camera because it had run its course. He returned to the first-floor dining area to do so. Meanwhile, Chuck and I continued on the second floor.

We were in the dining area when I heard Brad coming back up the steps. He whispered my name to get my attention. I walked out of the dining room and toward the top of the steps where I could see him. I had my camera trained on him since he was talking to me. He informed me that the fully charged battery he had just placed in his camera was nearly drained in a matter of minutes. I asked him if he was serious and of course he was. I felt like something was about to happen.

With my camera still trained on Brad as he was coming up the stairs, I saw something moving to my right out of the corner of my eye. At the same time, I could see the camera that was trained on the bathroom power down again. I turned my head and saw a six-foot-tall, solid black, three-dimensional silhouette of a man walking behind the bar for about two seconds before vanishing.

I lost my mind and I quickly turned the camera around in hopes of capturing the apparition on film. My excitement startled the other two investigators. Brad was on the stairs and could not see the bar area from that angle. Chuck was standing behind me, looking into the dining room. It was not until I jumped and cursed, staring at the bar, that they quickly looked in the same direction.

I could barely even speak. They were attempting to get out of me what had caught my attention. After I paced around the bar area for a few minutes, I finally calmed down enough to describe to them exactly what I saw. I re-created it, showing them exactly where the figure had walked behind the bar.

As I was talking, Chuck stopped me, noting that his camera battery was now drained. As he was telling us this, Brad and I had our backs to the bar, and then Chuck saw a shadow walk from the edge of the bar behind us. Although he admitted that what he saw was not quite as clear as my encounter, it startled him enough to spout, "What the hell was that?"

Once the excitement died down, I attempted to review my camera footage, hoping I had caught at least a glimpse of this shadow man on film. Unfortunately I had not; I looked before my camera did. This would lead me to invest in a head-mounted camera, which I now wear constantly. Wherever I look, it looks. Hopefully there will never be another case where I see something the camera did not because I could not get the camera around in time.

I was upset that I was unable to capture what I saw on film. I kept telling myself I still had decent footage of the shadow entity walking out of the bathroom earlier. But what I'd just seen was much more vivid than that. It was very disheartening, and honestly I felt like I was going to cry out of disappointment.

What I saw walking behind that counter is still as clear to me today as it was the night I witnessed it. I said it then and I will say again now: seeing that full-body apparition in person and directly in front of me was one of the best experiences of my career as a paranormal researcher. Moments like that make all the long nights and endless hours of work worthwhile.

After the boys talked me down, I moved the camera that had been filming the restroom into the bar and focused it where I'd seen the shadow man. Once again I plugged it into a wall outlet for power, and once again it powered back on as if nothing had happened.

It was now 2:30 in the morning. We all agreed that the cameras needed fully charged batteries, so we headed back downstairs to the first-floor dining area where all of our equipment was. All three of us placed fully charged batteries back on our handheld video cameras. While we were doing this, Brad turned his head in the direction of the lobby just outside of the dining room. He said he had heard a male voice coming from somewhere out there, maybe upstairs. We quickly headed back to the second floor.

As soon as we arrived on the second floor, I heard a loud thud come from downstairs. It seemed like whatever was there was starting to play games with us, the old cat-and-mouse routine. We went back down to the first floor. As we walked past the second dining area, I was blown away by the fact that the closet door was standing open once again. Somebody or something had moved the chair from in front of the door and put it back underneath the table I took it from, leaving the door wide open. I was amazed. Could that have been the thud I'd heard moments earlier?

We turned around to look into the bar and noticed a single wine bottle cork in the middle of the floor. We agreed that it was not there earlier, based on the fact that we all noticed it simultaneously and that it was something we would have kicked or tripped over at some point if it had been there. So now we had to figure out where it came from.

After a few moments of investigating the scene, Chuck pointed out an uncorked wine bottle on the bar. The cork we discovered in the middle of the floor matched it perfectly. Somehow the cork had come out of that bottle and onto the floor. Again, this was something that takes physical force to do. At this point, we were all wondering what we were going to find next.

We entered the kitchen again, where we were surprised to find that the dirty rags from the hamper had been dumped on the floor. The rags were right in view and directly in the traffic path. This was also something that we would have seen, kicked, and tripped over a number of times, had they been there earlier in the night. I even reviewed the video footage from each time we'd been in the kitchen. The footage showed that the rags were in the hamper.

The night kept getting better and better. The paranormal activity that we had experienced in just a few hours was astonishing. But we had yet to try to remove the picture in the men's restroom. We were told that the activity heightened when it was moved.

We went to get the picture and took it into the first-floor bar. Obviously no lights flickered upon removing it from the wall, since there were no lights on to begin with. I placed the picture on a wooden table. Immediately, the magnetic pickup on my chest started registering an audible electromagnetic field. For some strange reason, the picture was giving off an electromagnetic field that we could hear through my amplifier.

The field quickly moved and I was able to track it a few feet away from the table. Then it started moving again—this time toward Brad, who was filming the scene. I set my camera down on the bar and started following the field solely with my magnetic pickup. As it moved closer to Brad, the reading of the EMF tester in Chuck's hand started to rise. We were standing right in front of Brad when the camera I had placed on the bar powered down right beside us. Then the field was gone.

Chuck placed his EMF tester on the picture. Immediately the reading spiked to a fourteen on the Tesla scale. A wooden table and an old picture wouldn't ordinarily give off such a high electromagnetic field, so it was really something to witness. I asked out loud if the man in the picture was him, referring to the ghost. On cue, the meter jumped to a twenty-two, then back down to a steady fifteen. This was incredible.

Finally I said I was going to make a deal. I told the entity that I would put the picture back if he would do something for us to prove he was really present. No sooner did I say that than Brad's camera, which was documenting the activity, went dead. The camera was drained of battery life once again. Keeping my word, I placed the picture back in the men's restroom and we regrouped in the dining room where our equipment was.

The three of us were once again placing fully charged batteries back on our cameras and discussing how none of us had ever been in a location that caused so many battery drains. It was uncanny. After charging the gear up, we walked back into the first-floor bar. I immediately checked for any electromagnetic fields around that wooden table now that the picture had been removed. The detector registered 0.01. Whatever had been there was now gone.

We went back out into the hall and started walking toward the lobby when Chuck stopped cold in his tracks. He turned his head back toward me to ask if I had just heard a voice. I had. We both had heard what sounded like a female sighing coming from the second floor. This, of course, prompted us to investigate.

As we were nearing the top of the stairs, Chuck said that he had shivers going up and down his spine. I acknowledged the coldness of the area. We crept across the bar area, toward where the stationary camera was filming. Right in front of us, it once again powered down, even though it was plugged into an outlet. The handheld video camera in Chuck's hand did as well.

The two cameras powered down completely at the same time, and along with the significant temperature change, I felt like something was going to happen. I quickly turned the stationary camera back on to review the videotape. We stood there in awe as we heard a voice come across. It said, "What are you doing?" We were stunned.

The time was approximately 3:30. All three of us sat down in the bar to discuss the investigation so far. We all acknowledged the fact that this had been the most active location any of us had ever had the privilege of researching. Ironically, the next hour produced no activity for us to document. It seemed like the activity ceased right around three in the morning; it was just before one in the morning when it started. A solid two hours of nonstop paranormal activity is something to cherish. On a normal case, you are lucky to experience one or two events during an entire night. In most cases, those few things you did experience can easily be disproved. The Brentwood Wine Bistro broke that rule into a million pieces.

At 4:30, we packed up all of the gear and locked up the bistro. I was surprised to see snow outside, since the east coast of South Carolina rarely sees any. That was just another oddity to add to the night's long list of oddities.

I called the owners the following morning and reported to them about our experiences. Then I spent the next two days reviewing all of the material, over and over again, just to be sure there was not some logical explanation we'd missed in our excitement. I placed all of the video captures into one file for the owners to view. Needless to say, they were more than pleased. I believe they found comfort in knowing that what was happening in the bistro was not all in their minds.

I did not sleep for days following that initial investigation; the excitement of it was still pumping through my veins. Without hesitation, I scheduled a follow-up investigation.

———————

I contacted my friends at the Brentwood to set up another night of investigative work and they welcomed my request. This time, I felt the need to bring more investigators. Maybe they would find something I did not, or disprove something I previously felt was authentic paranormal activity. I invited members from the North Carolina Division of the P.I.T. Crew and also brought in a few from my core team in South Carolina.

We all met outside of the Brentwood around 10:30 at night. I could tell by the look on everyone's faces that they were excited to get started inside a place they had heard so much about. Once again we used the first dining room to the right as our base of operations.

I spoke with the owners to catch up on any activity that had occurred since my last visit. Sure enough, they had experienced a few unexplainable incidents. They told me about going into the attic and briefly witnessing a solid shadow figure shoot past them. They also heard a light sound from across the attic, as if something were moving or scuffling about. The attic was an area I hadn't yet researched; previously, there hadn't been any reason to. Neither the owners nor staff spend much time up there, so there were no claims concerning that area. Now there were, so tonight I planned to spend some time up there, and I'm glad I did.

After scouring the entire location to make sure all investigators were clear on everything, I decided to split us up into three separate groups: two investigators stationed in the first-floor bar area, and two others in the kitchen area; leaving me and one other to venture into the attic, where the most recent paranormal occurrences had taken place. I made sure to keep a floor between us so we did not contaminate one another's potential evidence. The time was a little after midnight when we all went our separate ways.

The attic entrance was your typical pull-down ladder design. My partner, who I'll call Derek, entered first with me directly behind him. The attic was huge, spanning the entire length of the house, and was stacked full of extra chairs, tables, and random junk. It was very well lit from the outside lighting that remained on each night and shone through the windows. The heat up there hit us like a ton of bricks; we logged a temperature of ninety-four degrees Fahrenheit. It was summer, so we had expected that.

We were not but a few feet into the attic when the activity started. The tape recorder in the left pocket of my vest mysteriously turned on by itself. I was filming at the time, so I had a record of this on the camera's audio. As soon as the tape recorder started to play, I unzipped my pocket and pulled it out. At first it was playing only the hissing sound that a blank tape makes. Then all of a sudden a male voice came from the speaker, saying, "Wednesday, November eighteenth." The voice was very serious, as if it were logging a date of importance. It reminded me of when a coroner begins his or her recording before performing an autopsy.

Both Derek and I were taken aback by this. I immediately stopped the tape player and rewound it back a few seconds. To our surprise, the voice we had just heard was not on the tape. Something had used the magnetic tape and audio recorder to communicate a date to us.

Immediately following this, I heard a gasping sound coming from directly below the attic entrance. Derek heard it too. I called one of the downstairs investigators on the two-way radio to confirm that nobody was on the second floor. She confirmed that everybody was on the first floor and no one had been on the second floor since we split up. Derek replied by saying, "Rock and roll!" I agreed. Within a matter of minutes after entering the attic, we'd captured two phantom voices on my handheld video camera. The night was looking very promising.

Meanwhile, the two investigators I'd instructed to examine the first-floor bar had not made it there yet. Instead, they took a detour to examine the first-floor men's restroom where the infamous creepy picture hung, the one I mentioned earlier that causes activity when moved. While they were in the restroom, they decided to conduct a brief communication session. Their goal was to capture electronic voice phenomena on their audio recorders. One of the investigators asked what the entities' names were. We later discovered on his audio recorder that two separate answers were given. One was a female voice that openly gave a name. The other was a male voice that said "No," as if to refuse the question. Following this session, the two investigators went to the bar area to conduct research there.

In the kitchen area, the remaining two investigators were busy conducting their own communication session by using magnetic alphabet letters on one of the food preparation tables. They had little success.

In the attic, Derek and I stationed ourselves in the center of the room on a couple of chairs. We started a full communication session, and after about fifteen minutes we started to hear something moving toward the back of the attic. It was darker in that area so we could not see what was moving. Derek kept asking questions aloud. He finally asked if whatever was there could make a knocking sound. Immediately we both heard, very clearly, a single knock in response. We knew something was there, and whatever it was knew we were there.

Both Derek and I noticed that the ambience of the room started to change drastically. The once hot and humid area had now cooled off to a very comfortable temperature, and the visibility had changed significantly. When we first arrived, the area was very well lit from the outside lighting. Now, the light had dimmed drastically, leaving only a nearly perfect circle of light around us. Where we could once see smoke detectors and electrical work on the walls, we now could not. Something was closing in around us.

We continued on with the communication session by placing one of our flashlights on the plywood floor. I asked if whatever was there could make the flashlight turn on. I received no response to numerous attempts. However, when I went to pick up the flashlight, it turned on as bright as can be and started shorting out. (To this day, that flashlight remains inoperable.) I finally told the entity that I had seen it earlier, so there was no need to hide. I asked if he or she would come closer to us. As soon as I said that, I lost all power to my recording video camera.

Immediately afterward, the light in the attic began to brighten and return to its normal state. The heat in the room became evident again. Whatever was there had left us, and it was time for us to rejoin the others.

We left the attic and arrived back in the second-floor bar area. I noticed immediately that the handset of an antique telephone that hung on the wall was dangling and swinging, as if somebody had just used it and walked away without hanging it up. I quickly referred back to video I had shot of the area earlier, and the footage confirmed that the handset was originally on its base. Something had moved it while we were in the attic.

We returned to the first floor. As we were standing in front of the restrooms, Derek was startled by something walking across the lobby. I did not see it, since I was facing the opposite direction. He was quick to dismiss it as being one of the other investigators walking into the dining area where all of our equipment was. I wanted to be sure, so I suggested we take a closer look.

Both of us walked out to where we could see the entire lobby and stood in silence. Every so often, we would hear what sounded like somebody clicking a pen. Soon one of the other investigators walked out into the lobby and we quickly asked him if he or anybody else had recently walked through there. He confirmed that no one had; they all had been back in the kitchen for quite some time.

We told him what we had just been experiencing as the rest of the investigators joined us in the lobby area. One of them noted that earlier in the night he too had heard what sounded like a pen clicking. Upon entering the first dining area, another investigator noted that a click pen he had on one of the tables was now missing. Could this have been the sound that several of us had heard?

The team showed a lot of excitement as Derek and I told about our experiences in the attic, and about Derek having seen a shadow figure walking through the lobby. The time was now 12:59. We had not been investigating all that long and we had experienced quite a lot of activity in a very short period.

As the entire team was standing in the lobby, a very loud alarm sound came out of nowhere. At first I thought one of us had accidently tripped the bistro's security system, the sound was so loud. We quickly located the actual source of the alarm. In between the baluster posts on the stairs sat a small alarm clock. It was covered in dust and cobwebs and appeared not to have been touched in a very long time. I grabbed it to take a closer look. The alarm was going off at one in the morning exactly. This was interesting, since during the previous investigation, the activity started to increase around that time. I shut off the alarm and placed the clock back where I had found it.

Next, we decided to investigate the third dining area on the first floor, where we all took note of the beautiful antique record player. Another investigator and I started messing with it to see if we could get it to work. Sure enough, we did, and to our surprise, it played a Christmas song in June. Very odd, considering the owner later told me that he was unaware that the record player even worked. This room and the music would play a very important role during a later investigation.

Shortly after, all six of us met in the first-floor bar area to conduct a few experiments. We sat around a table and at the bar. Once again, we brought in the picture from the men's restroom and placed it on the table where the majority of us were sitting. On the table we had placed multiple EMF testers, K-2 meters, audio recorders, and tri-field meters. More than half of us were running hand-held video cameras to document the scene, and a few were also logging temperature changes.

We sat in complete darkness with the video cameras recording in infrared. I sat with the MV-1 goggles on, turning my head back and forth to cover all areas of the room. I could see nothing but total darkness at first, and of course the infrared lights on all the cameras. Then I started to notice a strange glow coming from the picture on the table. After a few minutes, it vanished. Seconds later, directly to my right, I saw a white arc about three feet in length, slowly moving. Although I could see these visual anomalies through the goggles, the rest of the investigators could see nothing. The K-2 meters and the EMF testers continued to register activity.

I was becoming disoriented wearing the goggles, so I asked Derek to take over. He put the goggles on and started visually panning across the room. Only a few moments had passed when he witnessed a white streak move from behind one of the other investigators. At the same time, the K-2 meter was lighting up like a Christmas tree. Whatever the anomaly was, it was giving off a lot of energy.

Moments after this, we all heard what sounded like a scuffing sound coming from out in the lobby. At first we thought it was one of our investigators scuffing his foot, but we were all sitting or standing still. A few seconds later, I clearly saw a black mass walk past the doorway and down the hall. I jumped up to investigate. We tried to re-create what I had seen by walking in front of the windows and shining lights behind one another to try and cast a shadow in that direction. But our shadows were too big to have caused what I had just seen.

Next, I wanted to return to the attic for a second look and took two others with me. Another investigator was the first to enter the attic, and he stopped suddenly when he saw something out of the ordinary. He quickly looked down at me and the other investigator to ask if anyone had moved anything up in the attic; both of us confirmed that we had not. But now the chairs that were previously stacked off to the side were blocking the main path through the attic. Something had purposely placed those chairs in the way so we would not go back in there. Needless to say, we moved the chairs and investigated for a while, but this time nothing paranormal was documented. The attic was quiet.

We returned to the first floor and met up with the other investigators. They reported hearing and documenting very low music coming out of nowhere for a few minutes. They described it as being dark, scary, orchestral music. Talk about adding a creepy element to an already creepy situation! They also reported hearing the lobby phone ring one time.

It was now 3:35 and the activity seemed to have stopped for the night. Just like the previous investigation, the activity was strongest from around one to three in the morning.

Upon returning to the dining area to start packing up our equipment, the investigator who had lost his pen found it sitting on one of his equipment cases as if someone had purposely placed it there. He noted that he had been in and out of that case all night and the pen was not there earlier. Another investigator started examining the alarm clock that went off at one in the morning. She noted that it actually had been set for eleven at night, another strange discovery to make note of. How could an alarm clock go off at a time different than what it had been set for? I guess that's why they call it paranormal.

We finished packing up the gear and locked the bistro tight as we exited. The six of us had experienced a lot of activity that evening, some of which was much different from the previous investigation.

Following that night, I spent more time researching the history of the original owners and the house itself. I was able to locate the original owners' gravesites, which were less than a mile from the Brentwood Wine Bistro. On a map, I was able to draw a perfect equilateral triangle from their gravesites to the original location of the house to where the house currently operates as a bistro. I'm not sure whether that is relevant to the case, but it certainly is interesting. I've always had a fascination with triangles; in fact, I have the Eye of Horus, or All-Seeing Eye, encased in a triangle tattooed on my left shoulder.

For the follow-up investigation, I called on Chuck, one of the members of the original investigation, as well as three of my North Carolina Division members. There were five of us set to research the building that evening.

After the bistro closed, we split into two groups and started investigating sections of the building apart from one another. During this time, not much occurred that could be deemed paranormal. We were all conducting communication sessions, which we later discovered had produced a few unexplainable voices on the audio recorders.

After about an hour, we regrouped in the second-floor bar area where we were all doing our own investigation work. Two investigators were sitting at the bar conducting a communication session, while the other two investigators were examining the neighboring dining areas. As this was occurring, I heard a voice coming from the first floor. I quietly approached the banister at the top of the stairs and peered over so I could see the first-floor lobby area and restroom entrance.

I heard a voice again; this time I could identify it as male and pinpoint it as coming from the restroom area. I stood there quietly watching and listening from the second floor. I did not bring this to the attention of the others. I had left my handheld video camera on the bar, filming the two investigators conducting the communication session. Now I was afraid that if I went back for it, I might miss the opportunity to document something extraordinary. I was right.

Luckily for me, I had a digital still-shot camera hanging around my neck and my MV-1 goggles on my head. I quietly lifted up the camera, flipped up the flash, and took a few shots of the area below. After a few shots, I turned off the flash and set the camera to shoot continuously. Then I placed the camera lens inside the MV-1 goggles. I had a gut feeling that something was going to come out of the restroom area, and if it was the shadow entity I had seen before, I did not want a flash washing him out. After all, a flash (and infrared, for that matter) is designed to take away the darkness. When we're dealing with a solid black mass, who wants to do that?

Soon I heard the male voice again and a slight creak, as though the restroom door had opened. I lifted the camera and held the button down until nearly two dozen shots had been taken. When I heard no further activity, I immediately started scrolling back through the images to see if I had caught anything of relevance. To my surprise, I had. My stomach sank and I began to feel lightheaded from excitement. I had captured the shadow entity in a photograph, as plain as day at the bottom of the stairs. You can see his head, shoulder, and body, all in solid black. He appeared just like a three-dimensional shadow and seemed to be walking down and into the lobby.

After staring at this image for a few moments, I got the attention of the other investigators. I wanted them to see it now to rule out any questions later about its authenticity. The image was an excellent capture and having four other individuals verify it on the spot was vital to its validity. They all were amazed.

At this point, we decided to relocate to the first floor since that was obviously where the entity was. As we reached the lobby, we were startled by the house telephone ringing—again, just once. I ran over and picked it up to see who was calling. According to the caller ID, the phone call had been made from inside the building. Something had called the house line from another phone inside. The phone rang at one in the morning, once again proving that around that time the activity begins to peak.

From the lobby, we could see down the hall and to the kitchen door. We noticed that the kitchen light was on, since we could see light coming from underneath the door. This was odd; we had left that room dark earlier. We ran back to investigate. It seemed as if the entity was leading us back to the kitchen, but we discovered nothing there to explain why.

We returned to the bar upstairs, where we discovered that two wine bottle corks had been placed on the piano in the bar. A cork was placed standing up at each end of the piano. Those corks had not been there previously, as our video documentation proved.

I decided to split the team up again to explore different sections of the bistro. This entity was intelligent and I figured the more ground we could cover at once, the better. Two investigators remained in the bar on the second floor while the rest of us returned to the first floor.

Chuck and I decided to conduct a communication session in the third dining room on the first floor, where the old record player was. The other investigator went to examine other areas of the first floor alone. We sat at a table and placed an audio tape recorder on it to document the communication session.

As we started to ask questions of the entity, Chuck asked if it could make itself known. Immediately the tape recorder stopped recording. This got my attention, so I kneeled down directly in front of it to document it with the video camera. I asked if the entity could make the recorder start up again. Right on cue, the recorder commenced recording. Then I asked if the entity could stop it. Right on cue, the recorder stopped recording.

Both of us were amazed at this interaction with the entity. Chuck grabbed the audio recorder and played it back to see if any disembodied voices had been captured. I placed one of my tape recorders on the table to document what he was doing. He rewound the tape and hit play. I could not believe what happened next. No disembodied voices were on the tape. Instead, after he hit the play button, a rock song from the 1960s started to come through the recorder's speaker.

This was impossible. The tape had been recording off and on during the entire session. We heard no music at the time and the tape was a blank. Yet following the interaction with the entity, an old song had been mysteriously placed on the recording. Uncanny is not even the word for it. The really unsettling part was the fact that our voices from the communication session we had just conducted were also present along with the song.

At this time, the third investigator entered the room and we told her of the activity. Then the two investigators from upstairs came into the dining room. They had returned to the first floor since one of them was feeling really uneasy about what had just happened upstairs. They had started to experience an extreme change in the room's temperature. The area where they were sitting grew bitterly cold, and they started to hear music coming from behind them.

They asked us if we had heard music a few moments earlier, and this prompted me to tell them what we had just experienced. I played them the tape to show that our voices were somehow mixed in with the old rock song. Then they explained that the music they had heard was not a rock song—it was a piano piece. I thought this was really interesting and decided to play the tape once more. Every single one of us was floored when this time, the music was not that 1960s rock song. This time, on the same tape after I hit play, piano music was present. This was absolutely amazing. We called it a night shortly after that.

The investigation was a career highlight for me. Capturing the shadow entity in a photograph was worth its weight in gold. The next day, I showed that photo to the owners of the bistro. I was extremely pleased when they said that was exactly what they had been seeing all this time. It was very gratifying. After eight months of research into their case, I had successfully captured a very clear image of their ghost.

————

Many pages ago, I mentioned seeing the face of a ghost in a mirror. That eerie encounter took place on my next visit to the Brentwood Wine Bistro—exactly one year to the day after first stepping foot inside the building. I believe that learning the building's ins and outs and building a relationship with its entities paid off. I believe that they have reached a certain level of comfort with me.

On a night in January 2011 that we were calling "the anniversary," one other investigator and I arrived at the Brentwood for another investigation. We did all the usual things that had become routine by now—setting up our equipment in the first dining area to the right, sweeping the building for baseline readings.

We decided to conduct a communication session on the second floor. We were working in the dining area adjacent to the bar where the shadow entity is often seen. A large mirror hung over top of the fireplace. Not long into this session, my partner, who I'll call Jack, reported witnessing a face come out of the mirror. At first I thought he was joking, but he insisted it was true. This led us to begin taking photographs throughout the room. One in particular stopped us in our tracks.

As I was reviewing the digital photos I had just taken, I noticed something out of place in one of them. In the

upper right-hand corner, there appeared to be a face looking back at us. I quickly showed Jack the picture and he
too thought it looked like a face. But viewing the image
on the two-inch screen of the camera was not doing it
justice. I was eager to get back to the office for a more
thorough review.

We headed back to the office with only one thing on
our minds: looking at that photo on a much larger screen.
Upon arrival, I wasted no time loading that image into
my computer. When I opened it up on the screen, my jaw
dropped and I exhaled what little breath I had in me. I
could not believe what I was seeing. It was not only a remarkable capture, but it was one of the best photographs of
a ghost I had ever seen. This was a one-in-a-million shot.

One year of exhausting research had proved that the
ghost inside the Brentwood Wine Bistro is in fact real.
Now we had a face to go with the all of the other documentation validating the authenticity of the haunting.
This one piece of evidence added so much more depth to
the case. Once again, the owners were astounded. Days
after I presented the photograph to them, they kept saying, "I still can't get over this."

The Brentwood is my holy grail of paranormal research.
Since I first set foot in the building, this case has been my
obsession. I have seen the entity within on numerous occasions with my own two eyes, and have even caught it on
film a few times. The case file on the bistro is by far the

largest I have. Although there are other locations—many in this book—that have produced extraordinary paranormal activity, the Brentwood has yet to be matched.

I truly appreciate the owners of the building coming to me with their concerns and allowing me to conduct such a large amount of work there. I hold them and the building in high regard. I have also enjoyed working with all the various investigators and researchers on this case.

Earlier, I mentioned that the bistro sits on Luck Avenue, which is appropriate since it has become my lucky four-leaf clover. (My rabbit's foot still does me good some times, too.) I don't know if it's actually luck, or chance, or simply being in the right place at the right time. But I consider myself lucky to have been the one responsible for placing the haunted Brentwood Wine Bistro on the paranormal map.

Epilogue

Paranormal research is a giant puzzle with the pieces scattered everywhere. Some vital pieces necessary to complete the entire picture are still missing, yet we patiently continue to search for them. Some pieces do not fit in the spot we think they should, and some are not what they look like at first glance. But until we complete the picture, we must consider that nothing is impossible.

I seek the truth about ghosts, and I will continue my work until I become the very thing I have been searching for all of these years. The life of a paranormal researcher can be exciting and tedious at the same time. There are many dead ends, and many nights of sitting in silence until the sun comes up without discovering anything remotely paranormal. In fact, the majority of the cases I have researched produced no paranormal activity. But still I persist.

When a person chooses to become a doctor or a nurse, he or she studies the human body. An electrician educates himself or herself on electricity. A physicist studies physics, and so on and so forth. A paranormal researcher has to know a little about all of those topics, and much more, in order to competently tackle any given case.

Paranormal research is not a one-night event. Only through repeated sessions, thorough research, and continued education can we begin to understand a case's true nature. I studied for years before conducting any fieldwork, and am proud to be one of the innovators in this discipline. My career as a paranormal investigator and researcher has been an exciting one thus far. The past fourteen years have opened my eyes and mind to a wide range of possibilities and realities, and I have made some discoveries that prove, through scientific means, that paranormal activity does in fact exist in our everyday life. I am fortunate to have a collection of credible audio, video, and still photography that documents these occurrences.

I may never see the day when this field is universally accepted, nor the day when all of the answers are revealed. I believe that there are two different types of people. There are those who choose to accept things as they are, leaving their questions unanswered, and there are those who choose to spend their lives searching for those answers. I am still actively seeking the reasons for the incident I experienced in 1987. But at least for myself, I have answered the question, "Do ghosts exist?" The answer to that is a resounding "Yes."

The cases I've shared in this book help validate the belief that spirits do actually walk the earth. I believe that the soul continues after the body dies. It is a personality and an awareness, independent of the human body. When I speak to you, I am not speaking to your human biological composition. I am speaking to your soul. Why should that change after your flesh and blood expires? I know that life after death, in whatever form it takes, does exist.

On average, they say approximately 150,000 people die each day. Just remember, when you turn off your bedside lamp each night, there is a good chance that ghosts may be watching you. The good news is, I am watching them.

GET MORE AT **LLEWELLYN.COM**

Visit us online to browse hundreds of our books and decks, plus sign up to receive our e-newsletters and exclusive online offers.

- **Free tarot readings • Spell-a-Day • Moon phases**
- **Recipes, spells, and tips • Blogs • Encyclopedia**
- **Author interviews, articles, and upcoming events**

GET SOCIAL WITH **LLEWELLYN**

Find us on Facebook
www.Facebook.com/LlewellynBooks

Follow us on
twitter™
www.Twitter.com/Llewellynbooks

GET BOOKS AT **LLEWELLYN**

LLEWELLYN ORDERING INFORMATION

Order online: Visit our website at www.llewellyn.com to select your books and place an order on our secure server.

Order by phone:
- Call toll free within the U.S. at 1-877-NEW-WRLD (1-877-639-9753)
- Call toll free within Canada at 1-866-NEW-WRLD (1-866-639-9753)
- We accept VISA, MasterCard, and American Express

Order by mail:
Send the full price of your order (MN residents add 6.875% sales tax) in U.S. funds, plus postage and handling to: Llewellyn Worldwide, 2143 Wooddale Drive Woodbury, MN 55125-2989

POSTAGE AND HANDLING:
STANDARD: (U.S. & Canada)
(Please allow 12 business days)
$25.00 and under, add $4.00.
$25.01 and over, FREE SHIPPING.

INTERNATIONAL ORDERS (airmail only):
$16.00 for one book, plus $3.00 for each additional book.

Visit us online for more shipping options.
Prices subject to change.

FREE CATALOG!

To order, call
1-877-NEW-WRLD
ext. 8236
or visit our
website

Ghost Under Foot
The Spirit of Mary Bell
KENNETH W. HARMON

Just weeks after settling into their new home in Fort Collins, Colorado, retired police officer Kenneth W. Harmon and his family make a chilling discovery: they're living with a ghost.

This true haunting story begins during a ghost tour at the famous Stanley Hotel, where the Harmons experienced headaches and paranormal activity. Once back home, strange rapping noises, eerie whispers captured on film, and unidentified dark shapes in his photographs compel Ken to research the land's history. What he learns shocks everyone: in the backyard sits the unmarked grave of Mary Bell Winston, a young woman who died of typhoid fever in the late 1880s.

As his fixation grows, Ken uses a dowsing rod to communicate with Mary Bell's spirit and investigate her brief life. The spirit's surprising answers shed light on mysteries of the spirit world, crossing over, heaven and hell, and God.

978-0-7387-3081-3, 288 pp., 5³⁄₁₆ x 8   **$15.95**

To order, call 1-877-NEW-WRLD
Prices subject to change without notice
Order at Llewellyn.com 24 hours a day, 7 days a week!

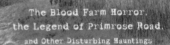

Marcus F. Griffin
Foreword by Jeff Belanger

EXTREME
PARANORMAL
I N V E S T I G A T I O N S

The Blood Farm Horror,
the Legend of Primrose Road,
and Other Disturbing Hauntings

Extreme Paranormal Investigations
The Blood Farm Horror, the Legend of Primrose Road, and Other Disturbing Hauntings
Marcus F. Griffin

Set foot inside the bone-chilling, dangerous, and sometimes downright terrifying world of extreme paranormal investigations. Join Marcus F. Griffin, Wiccan priest and founder of Witches in Search of the Paranormal (WISP), as he and his team explore the Midwest's most haunted properties. These investigations include the creepiest-of-the-creepy cases WISP has tackled over the years, many of them in locations that had never before been investigated. These true case files include investigations of Okie Pinokie and the Demon Pillar Pigs, the Ghost Children of Munchkinland Cemetery, and the Legend of Primrose Road. Readers will also get an inside glimpse of previously inaccessible places, such as the former Jeffrey Dahmer property as WISP searches for the notorious serial killer's spirit, and the farm that belonged to Belle Gunness, America's first female serial killer and the perpetrator of the Blood Farm Horror.

978-0-7387-2697-7, 264 pp., 5³⁄₁₆ x 8   **$15.95**

To order, call 1-877-NEW-WRLD
Prices subject to change without notice
Order at Llewellyn.com 24 hours a day, 7 days a week!

OVER 1000 HAUNTED PLACES YOU CAN EXPERIENCE

THE GHOST HUNTER'S FIELD GUIDE

RICH NEWMAN

The Ghost Hunter's Field Guide
Over 1,000 Haunted Places You Can Experience
RICH NEWMAN

Ghost hunting isn't just on television. More and more paranormal investigation groups are popping up across the nation. To get in on the action, you need to know where to go.

The Ghost Hunter's Field Guide features over 1,000 haunted places around the country in all fifty states. Visit battlefields, theaters, saloons, hotels, museums, resorts, parks, and other sites teeming with ghostly activity. Each location—haunted by the spirits of murderers, Civil War soldiers, plantation slaves, and others—is absolutely safe and accessible.

This indispensable reference guide features over 100 photos and offers valuable information for each location, including the tales behind the haunting and the kind of paranormal phenomena commonly experienced there: apparitions, shadow shapes, phantom aromas, telekinetic activity, and more.

978-0-7387-2088-3, 432 pp., 6 x 9   **$17.95**

To order, call 1-877-NEW-WRLD
Prices subject to change without notice
Order at Llewellyn.com 24 hours a day, 7 days a week!

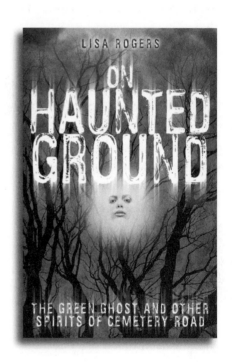

On Haunted Ground
The Green Ghost and Other Spirits of Cemetery Road
LISA ROGERS

Lisa Rogers sensed that the house she bought with her husband Wes came with a ghost. But nothing prepared them for doors slamming on their own, objects flying, and the nightly appearance of a freaky green orb in their bedroom. Their two children had opposing views on the paranormal activity. While Keshia grew attached to the grandmotherly ghost who taught her not to be afraid of thunderstorms and the Native American spirit that tucked her into bed, her brother Troy wasn't so quick to believe in their unearthly guests.

This amazing true story details two decades of terrifying, funny, and heartwarming paranormal encounters—the mischievous entity that imitated the voice of each family member, the spool that "came to life" to chase the kids, the shocking events that shook Wes and Troy's skepticism—and the enduring love that keeps the family together through it all.

978-0-7387-3236-7, 264 pp., 5³⁄₁₆ x 8   **$15.95**

To order, call 1-877-NEW-WRLD
Prices subject to change without notice
Order at Llewellyn.com 24 hours a day, 7 days a week!

VIVIAN CAMPBELL

STALKED
by
SPIRITS

true tales of a ghost magnet

Stalked by Spirits
True Tales of a Ghost Magnet
Vivian Campbell

Haunted since childhood, Vivian Campbell has encountered angry wraiths, mischievous child spirits, terrorizing demons, and all sorts of bizarre, unearthly beings. Vivian relives these chilling and thrilling experiences in *Stalked by Spirits*, including how she and her family suffered violent phantom attacks, received small favors from a little girl ghost, negotiated with a demanding spirit, welcomed back a dearly departed pet, tolerated ghostly attendance at holiday dinners and Girl Scout meetings, and waged hair-raising battles with an evil entity threatening their baby daughter.

Taking us inside a variety of spirit-infested, often beautiful places—a stone mansion in the Tennessee mountains, a century-old college dorm, the first apartment she shared with her new husband, and the beloved Florida home that's been in her family for generations—these true tales vividly capture an extraordinary and haunted life.

978-0-7387-2731-8, 288 pp., 5³⁄₁₆ x 8   **$15.95**

To order, call 1-877-NEW-WRLD
Prices subject to change without notice
Order at Llewellyn.com 24 hours a day, 7 days a week!